Creating Storytellers and Writers

II CREATING STORYTELLERS AND WRITERS

Creating Storytellers and Writers

(for 5-12 year-olds)

Pie Corbett and Julia Strong

IV CREATING STORYTELLERS AND WRITERS

Talk for Writing
15 Branch Street
Huddersfield
West Yorkshire
HD1 4JL

Contact Nick Batty at contact@talk4writing.com
01484 280165
www.talk4writing.com

First published, 2017

Copyright   ©Pie Corbett and Julia Strong

All rights reserved. The handouts within this book may be reprinted to support in-school training only, but they remain the intellectual property of Pie Corbett and Julia Strong and are subject to copyright. It is forbidden to use the handouts for commercial gain, place them on the internet or share them with other schools or institutions. Except for the handouts and the use of brief extracts for review purposes, no part of this publication may be reproduced or transmitted in any form or by any means, electronic or mechanical, including photocopy, recording, or any information and retrieval system, without permission in writing from the publisher (Talk for Writing) or a license from the Copyright Licensing Agency Ltd, Barnard's Inn, 86 Fetter Lane, London EC4A 1EN (www.cla.co.uk).

ISBN: 978-1-9998942-2-1

British Library Cataloguing in Publication Data
A catalogue record of this book is available from the British Library

- Typeset and printed by deltaleeds.co.uk
- Conference film clips by quickstepfilms.com
- DVDs produced by imgfactory.co.uk
- Icons designed by jonralphs.com
- Cover design by www.knownaim.co.uk
- Photographs: Julia Strong & Talk for Writing Training Schools

This book is available for purchase from Roving Books. Tel: 01455 822192
Email: hello@rovingbooks.com

Dedication

Creating Storytellers and Writers is dedicated to all the teachers and consultants who have contributed to the development of Talk for Writing across the years. In particular, we would like to thank all the Talk for Writing Training Schools without whose help this book could not have been written. These schools can all be visited to see the process in action and they and the Talk for Writing consultants can be contacted to provide training. Visit www.talkforwriting.com/training

Pie Corbett and Julia Strong

Many thanks to Front Lawn Academy (Havant), Hallsville Primary (Newham) and Penn Wood Primary (Slough) for permission to use the pictures on the front cover of this book.

About the authors

Pie Corbett is an inspirational trainer, poet, author and editor of over 250 books, including the bestselling *Jumpstart! Literacy*. A former teacher, headteacher, lecturer and English inspector, he is famous in the education world for developing the transformational Talk for Writing approach.

Julia Strong, former English teacher, deputy headteacher and deputy director of the National Literacy Trust, now focuses on developing the Talk for Writing approach. She is an inspirational trainer for secondary schools, and the author of a number of bestselling books including *Talk for Writing Across the Secondary Curriculum*.

Pie and Julia have co-authored the following books:

- *Talk for Writing in the Early Years* (Open University Press, 2016)
- *Talk for Writing Across the Curriculum* (Open University Press, 2011 & 2017)
- *Jumpstart! Grammar* (David Fulton, 2014 & 2016)
- *Creating Storytellers and Writers* (Talk for Writing, 2017)

Index

Chapter 1: Introduction to Talk for Writing — 3
Overview of the Talk for Writing process — 5

Initial assessment — 7

Chapter 2: Imitation — 13
- Warming up the words — 13
- Internalising the text — 18
- Reading as a reader — 21
- Reading as a writer — 23
- Boxing up — 23
- Toolkits — 25
- Making learning visible — 30

Chapter 3. Innovation — 33
- Shared planning – boxing up the innovation — 33
- Shared writing – innovating on the model — 35
- Moving away from the model – levels of innovation — 38
- Children plan and write their own version — 43
- Peer assessment — 44
- Next steps based on assessment — 44

Chapter 4. Independent application and real independence — 47
- Was the writing effective? — 48
- The end of unit assessment – assessing progress — 50
- Achieving real independence through creativity and invention — 52

Resources — 55
Appendix 1. Teacher's notes — 56
Appendix 2. Toolkits for the 6 key story features — 76

Index of handouts
Handout 1: The Talk for Writing process — 89
Handouts 2a/2b: Overview of planning (Y3–4 & Y5–6) — 90
Handout 3: Talk for Writing progression document — see web ref page 2
Handout 4: Formative assessment — 92
Handouts 5a/5b: Boxing up the structure of the key story types (KS1/KS2) — 99
Handout 6: Model text examples — 109
Handout 7: Actions for the key sentence signposts — 116
Handout 8: The art of linking text — 117
Handout 9: Useful phrases for shared writing — 119
Handout 10: The art of shared writing — 121
Handout 11: Peer assessment sentence starters — 122
Handout 12: Levels of innovation — 123

Index of video clips

DVD 1	Clip 1: Introducing the underlying principles of Talk for Writing
	Clip 2: Talk for Writing overview
Chapter 1: Introduction	Clip 3: Initial assessment
	Clip 4: Initial assessment for early years
	Clip 5: Planning a unit
Chapter 2: Imitation stage	Clip 6: The hook
	Clip 7: Warming up and embedding grammar and spelling
	Clip 8: Warming up the tune of the text
	Clip 9: Teachers warming up the words at Warren Road Primary, Orpington
	Clip 10: Pupil demonstrating the difference it makes
	Clip 11: Imitating the model text
	Clip 12: Advice on how to help children imitate the model
	Clip 13: Examples of children storytelling
	Clip 14: Why internalising text matters
	Clip 15: Modelling how to text map and express a story
	Clip 16: The importance of teaching connectives and related actions
	Clip 17: Oral independent retelling
DVD 2	Clip 18: Introducing the written version of the text
	Clip 19: Reading as a reader – vocabulary
	Clip 20: Reading as a reader – comprehension
	Clip 21: Reading as a reader – booktalk
	Clip 22: Reading as a reader – overview of strategies
	Clip 23: Reading as a writer – boxing up
	Clip 24: Reading as a writer – co-constructing the writing toolkit
	Clip 25: Making the learning visible
Chapter 3: Innovation stage	Clip 26: Shared planning (simple substitution for early years)
	Clip 27: Shared planning (boxing up the plan and talking the new text)
	Clip 28: Shared writing illustrating hugging closely
	Clip 29: More advanced shared writing
	Clip 30: Planning a week's shared, guided and independent writing and editing
	Clip 31: Different levels of innovation to move towards real independence
	Clip 32: Two year 5 boys from Selby Primary School discussing writing
	Clip 33: Overview of moving into writing, with a focus on marking
	Clip 34: Making the marking lead to editing
Chapter 4: Independent application	Clip 35: Independent application
	Clip 36: Opportunities for free creative writing
	Clip 37: Summary of the Talk for Writing process

Chapter 1: Introducing Talk for Writing

> *Talk for Writing has helped me to sort out my thinking. I know how to write well now.* – year 4 pupil, Burnley Brow Primary School, Oldham

Talk for Writing is based on how children learn. It places the learner, through formative assessment, at the heart of the planning, teaching and learning process. The term Talk for Writing not only describes all the talk that surrounds the teaching of writing but also the wider learning within a unit. It helps the children become better speakers, listeners, readers, writers and thinkers. It includes the way in which an effective teacher thinks aloud, articulating thought processes as well as demonstrating readerly and writerly approaches. The children are engaged in talking through ideas and refining their spoken and written expression. By involving them in explaining to others, it enables the children to develop their understanding of whatever is being studied. And, of course, in the process it improves the children's reading: the more familiar you become with the tune of a text, the easier it is to read that sort of text because the generic language patterns have been internalised.

The underpinning Talk for Writing process moving from **imitation** through **innovation** into **independent application** can be applied to any type of writing, but this book focuses on fiction writing. The imitation stage is centred around getting the children to learn a story orally which enables a child to internalise a narrative pattern so that it is added to their linguistic repertoire. As Pie outlines in **video clips 1 & 2**, the teacher creates a memorable, meaningful version of the text type being taught (pitched just above the level where the children are), building in the structure and age-appropriate language features.

The children are then taken on a journey from imitation to innovation to independent application for each of the key story types. For an overview

4 CREATING STORYTELLERS AND WRITERS

of the structure of the key story patterns for KS1 and KS2 see **Handouts 5a and 5b** alongside **video clip 22**. The approach has not only proved to be transformational in raising standards in schools where it has been applied systematically but, most importantly, children love it:

> *When Pie Corbett invented story maps, it helped me with my writing because when I write in my book, I always know what to write.*
> – Jaime, aged 9, St George's School, Battersea, London

> *It's really good for the children in our class who can't hear very well or talk very well because of all the actions and sign language we use. We can all join in. It gives me lots of ideas about my writing because it's sometimes hard to think by myself and it doesn't make sense. I like it best when we do quizzes about our text.*
> – Kai from the SEND Harbour Centre, Staines

> *Story maps help me with my writing because I always have a bank of words to use.*
> – Yusra, 8, St George's Primary School, Battersea, London

> *I also find it helpful actually saying the words so I know what kind of words I can use for my own writing. It's amazing how much I've improved my writing, though I can't spell every word.*
> – Pupil from Sheffield Talk for Writing project

> *I really like Talk for Writing because I used to not like Literacy that much, but now I really do because I know what I am doing. I used to not have many ideas, but now I have lots. I also didn't know how to write my ideas down, how to format them, but now, with the help of the story maps, I have learnt how to get them onto the paper.*
> – Pupil from Warren Road Primary, Orpington

Parents are also very enthusiastic about it:

> *The difference in my son's abilities, awareness of language and different text types used now (he's in year 1) from such an early age, has been born from Talk for Writing. It has given him a much stronger start to writing. A love of writing is being fostered and the transition between year groups over time should become easier. What he can do and tell me at 6 years old is remarkable! Thank you for all your hard work and dedication in moving this initiative forward at Warren Road.*

This DVD focuses on helping children become confident speakers and writers in English but, of course, the same approach can be used to build confidence in

INTRODUCING TALK FOR WRITING 5

communication in any language – the picture here shows Talk for Writing in action in China. It is just a question of adapting it to fit the patterns of the language being focused on. Talk for Writing is starting to be used across the world.

Overview of the Talk for Writing process

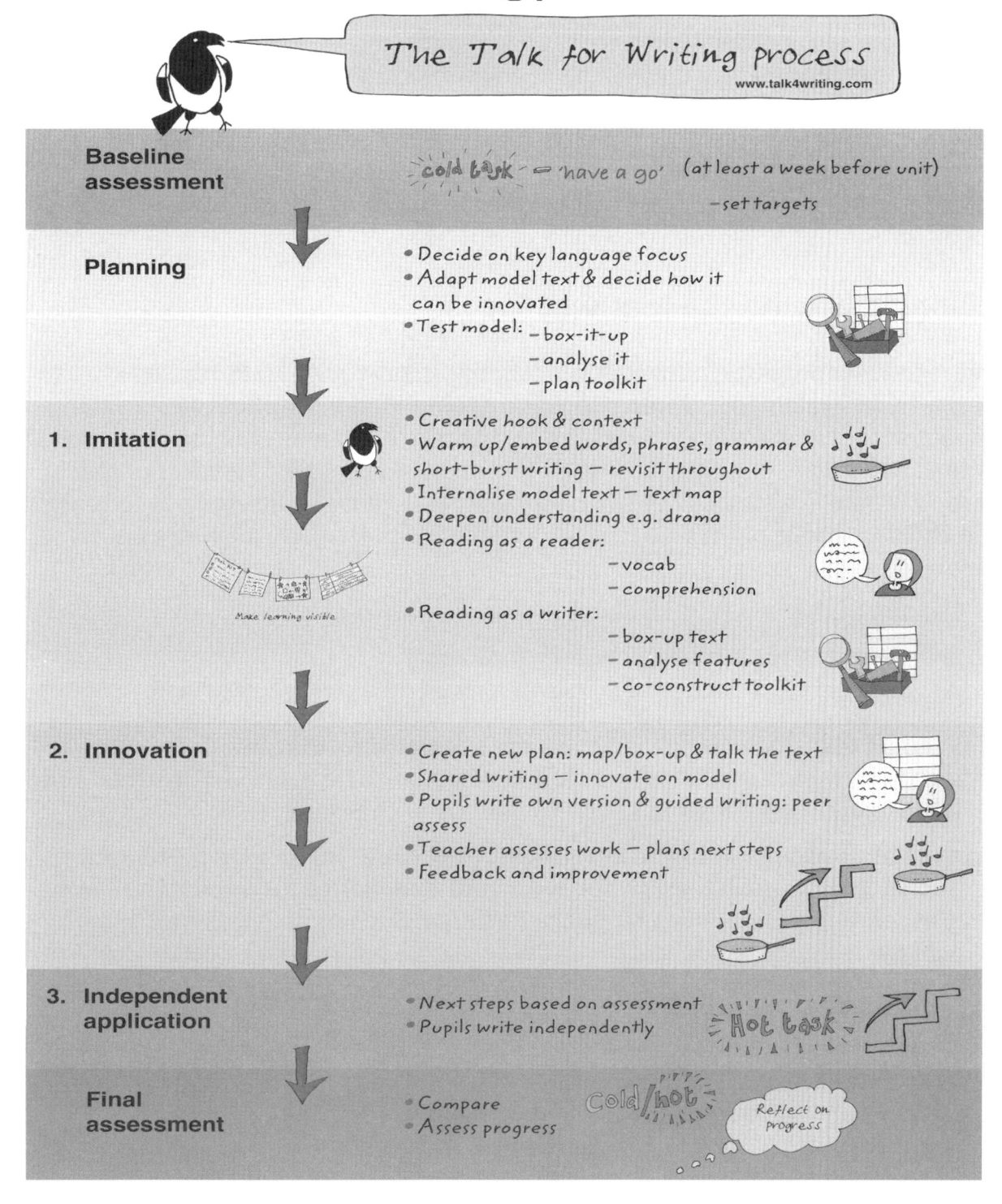

The Talk for Writing process
www.talk4writing.com

Baseline assessment
- cold task – 'have a go' (at least a week before unit)
- set targets

Planning
- Decide on key language focus
- Adapt model text & decide how it can be innovated
- Test model: – box-it-up
  – analyse it
  – plan toolkit

1. Imitation
- Creative hook & context
- Warm up/embed words, phrases, grammar & short-burst writing – revisit throughout
- Internalise model text – text map
- Deepen understanding e.g. drama
- Reading as a reader:
  – vocab
  – comprehension
- Reading as a writer:
  – box-up text
  – analyse features
  – co-construct toolkit

Make learning visible

2. Innovation
- Create new plan: map/box-up & talk the text
- Shared writing – innovate on model
- Pupils write own version & guided writing: peer assess
- Teacher assesses work – plans next steps
- Feedback and improvement

3. Independent application
- Next steps based on assessment
- Pupils write independently
- Hot task

Final assessment
- Compare
- Assess progress
- Cold/hot
- Reflect on progress

The Talk for Writing process is summed up by this poster (copies of which can be ordered from www.talkforwriting.co.uk/poster) or photocopied from **Handout 1**.

on page 83. Images from this poster are used as icons throughout the book to guide the reader. In **video clip 2**, Pie briefly illustrates the basic principles of Talk for Writing and its three stages moving from imitation to innovation to independent application. The theoretical essence is simple but practice is always more complex. The art of effective teaching is being able to identify where the children are on their learning journey and the skills they need next to make progress. Through planning well-focused units you can add to their repertoire through imitation and innovation so they can apply and develop these skills independently. In such a way, the children will achieve breadth and depth and will master flexible writing skills that can be adapted to suit the needs not only of any narrative writing task but writing in any subject. Moreover, the approach can be adapted to suit the needs of learners of all ages.

The accompanying DVDs illustrate this process in practice so you can see how to adapt it to the type of story text you want the pupils to be able to read, write or speak in.

Planning around the learning focus

Having a clear linguistic purpose for each unit is key to the child making progress, as explained in **video clip 5** and exemplified in **Handouts 2a and 2b**. If we are not careful, we get sidelined by the allure of an interesting topic like pirates and forget that the purpose of the unit is to use it as a vehicle to teach essential transferable skills through embedding language patterns not to teach the children about pirates. So, the wise teacher will think through the points below:

- the aim of the unit (e.g. to develop suspense writing skills)
- an interesting topic that will deliver that aim
- the hook that will engage the class with the topic
- a model text that will provide the linguistic patterns that the class will be shown how to reproduce. This model will need to be located or written and will usually need adapting to suit the needs of the class.
- a range of additional model texts illustrating these features in more depth and variety to provide extension work and a challenge for pupils who have grasped the underpinning language patterns. Such models will help pupils achieve real independence.

The difference it can make

Schools that have applied the approach systematically for several years have made excellent, in some cases even amazing, progress. For example:

- **St Matthew's** in Nechells, Birmingham, had dire results until the implementation of Talk for Writing. It has a challenging intake (87% pupil premium, 86% EAL and 18% SEND). In 2017, its results were as follows:

- Reading: 91% with 37% at greater depth; (National average: 71%)
- Writing: 90% with 23% at greater depth; (National average: 76%)
- Mathematics: 93% with 7% at greater depth. (National average: 75%)

- **St George's** in Battersea, London, had equally dire results until the implementation of Talk for Writing. It too has a challenging intake (48% pupil premium, 59% EAL and 17% SEND). In 2017, the school results were as follows:
  - Reading: 80% with 12% at greater depth;
  - Writing: 96% with 20% at greater depth;
  - Mathematics: 80% with 24% at greater depth.

Initial assessment:
– establishing the baseline and adjusting the model text

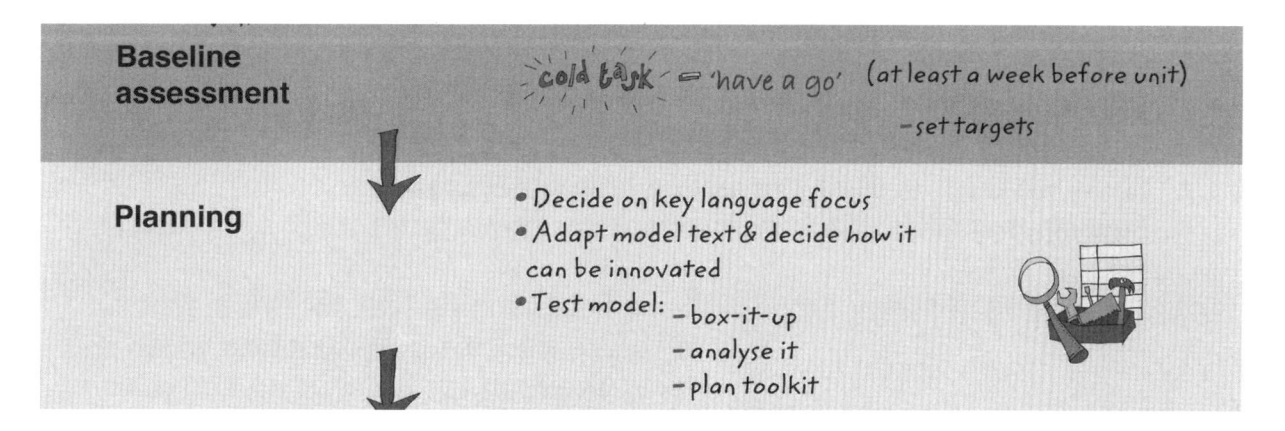

Baseline assessment	*cold task* = 'have a go' (at least a week before unit) – set targets

Planning	• Decide on key language focus
	• Adapt model text & decide how it can be innovated
	• Test model: – box-it-up
	    – analyse it
	    – plan toolkit

Look at the language aims for your year and establish where the children are on their learning journey. A useful document here is **Handout 3**, the Talk for Writing progression document, that you can download from www.talk4writing.co.uk/portfolio-items/year-on-year-progress/ and adapt to suit your school's curriculum. A good way of establishing exactly where children are on their learning journey is to set an activity to establish what **baseline skills** pupils already have in relation to the focus of a unit at least a week before beginning that unit. For younger pupils, you might want to call this Have a go! – the children's words could be recorded if they haven't started writing yet. For older pupils, we call it the ***cold task***, a term attributed to Roz Wilson.

The pupils will need a familiar context. For example, if the focus of the unit is characterisation, ask the children to think of a character, imaginary or real, and write a little story showing what they are like. This will give them something to write about that they know about and that interests them. Warm up the topic with a brief discussion but do not provide any teaching in how to write about this subject. This will help you pinpoint what specific skills to focus on in the unit to help the children progress. Pie illustrates this process for different age groups in **video clips 3 and 4**.

8 CREATING STORYTELLERS AND WRITERS

Look at the year 1 child's cold task writing below from Trevithick Primary, Cornwall:

Once there lived a orange and white clown fish. Called phoebe. She lived with her family. In some pink sparkling corell reef. But one day her little sisster got lost in the shipreck. Where a shark lived. She hast save her. But how.

If this were typical of writing in the class, the teacher would then know that the unit had to focus on some of the basic writerly techniques for effective characterisation as summed up in the following toolkit:

Characterisation toolkit
– To make your character come alive, you could:

- Describe the setting where main character (MC) is
    – use a preposition to place the setting
- Select effective adjectives to describe MC
- Include a striking fact about MC
- Tell reader about a hobby of MC
- Use a powerful verb to show how MC moves
- Show what MC is like by revealing how others react
- Reveal what MC is like by what they say (show don't tell)

So, a key planning task for the teacher is to use the cold task to decide what language features to focus on and plan the toolkit that will later be co-constructed with the class. The teacher makes this focus very explicit, as illustrated here from a washing line at Montgomery Academy, Birmingham.

For the first unit on any key writing focus that the children need to experience, for example dialogue, the teacher would prepare how to co-construct a simple, visual toolkit with the class. When dialogue is then a feature of a later unit, the teacher would plan to build on the existing toolkit, perhaps after establishing how much of it the class remembers.

At the same time, in any unit, you will be introducing or embedding some non-negotiable language features as appropriate to the age and attainment of your class. Therefore, what stage you are at in developing the everyday writing toolkit also needs to be planned. The example below would be for KS2 where the skills listed would be being embedded:

INTRODUCING TALK FOR WRITING

Everyday writing toolkit

- Write in sentences knowing where the sentences end
- Link sentences effectively
- Include a variety of sentence structures
- Use a variety of hook-your-reader techniques
- Use appropriate punctuation avoiding comma splices
- Check your spelling

Toolkits are fully explained on pages 25–29 and exemplified in detail in **Appendix 2**.

The hot task to demonstrate progress

At the end of the unit, the children would be asked to do a similar piece of characterisation writing, known as the *hot task*, when the children can show what they know. By comparing the cold and hot tasks, you can assess the progress made. The child who wrote the cold task above, wrote this as her hot task at the end of the unit:

Deep in the salty sea inside a pink corl reef there lived a clown fish. Covered in orange glowing scals and dazzling wite strips. She was the mst glamorus fiish in the entire oshen. Day after day she wood wiz threw the waves clecting crabs for her tea. So amazed at her rosted crabs the other fish wood ask "Please can we have a crab for are tea?" but Phoebe wood snap "No they are all mine!"

When you look at this writing, you can see that the teacher has focused on all the characterisation features mentioned in the planning for the toolkit on the previous page. If this were a model text, colour coding the different techniques used is a good way of turning the model into a toolkit with a class, once the class has analysed the model, because the colour coding can be done with the children's help in front of them, and is a useful visual aid.

Labels (left)	Text	Labels (right)
Describe setting + **preposition**	*Deep in the salty sea,* **inside** *a pink coral reef,* there lived a clown fish covered in orange, glowing scales and **dazzling**-white stripes. She was the most glamorous fish in the entire ocean. Day after day, she wood whizz through the waves collecting crabs for her tea. Amazed at her roasted crabs, the other fish would ask, "Please can we have a crab for our tea?" but Phoebe would snap, "No, they are all mine!"	Effective **adjective** to describe MC
Striking fact about MC		Powerful verb to show how MC moves
A hobby of MC		
Revealing what MC is like by showing how reacts to others		Showing what MC is like by what they say

10 CREATING STORYTELLERS AND WRITERS

Bookending units with a cold and hot task

The idea is to bookend units of work with a cold and hot task so that the teacher, the child, the parents and anyone visiting the class can easily see the progress made within the unit – as illustrated by **video clip 3**. It is also worth looking at **Handout 4**. In many ways, this handout is an extended overview of the cold to hot process and shows how formative assessment is at the heart of effective teaching and learning.

It is useful to make it visually obvious in the children's books where the opening cold task baseline is and where the hot task is at the end of the unit. You might want to get the children to write on appropriately coloured paper, e.g. pale blue for cold and pale orange for hot and then stick the work in the books. An easier method, favoured by those who value their weekends, is to use coloured tabs or stamps – blue for the cold text, red for the hot – so anyone looking at the book can easily locate the start and end of each unit and identify the level of progress made.

The cold task enables the teacher to assess the work of the whole class and identify the key skills that the class already has and how these could be developed within the unit as well as any new skills to be introduced. These form the key targets throughout the unit. It might help to think of these targets as Rome and ensure that all roads lead there: all the activities planned help to introduce and embed the key skills covered by the unit. Also, note down specific skills that less confident writers will need more help with and opportunities where the skills of more confident writers could be extended.

In such a way, many teachers use assessing the cold task as an opportunity to set a few key achievable targets for each child for the unit, ensuring that these then feature in the ensuing warm-up work, the model text and the shared writing so that the child has a chance to understand how these skills work and then practise them themselves.

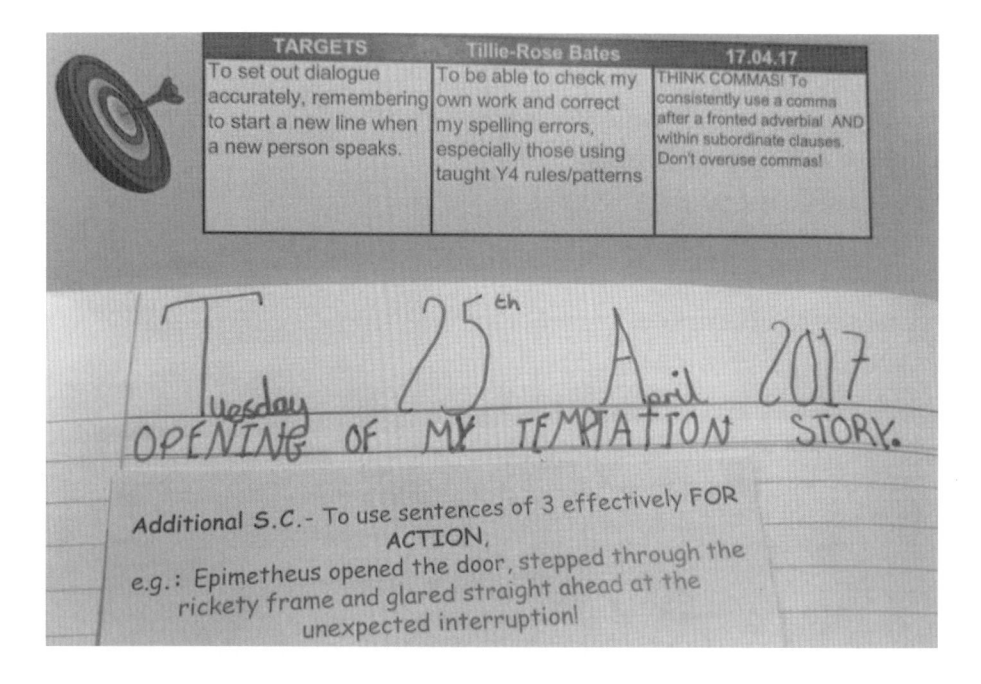

TARGETS	Tillie-Rose Bates	17.04.17
To set out dialogue accurately, remembering to start a new line when a new person speaks.	To be able to check my own work and correct my spelling errors, especially those using taught Y4 rules/patterns	THINK COMMAS! To consistently use a comma after a fronted adverbial AND within subordinate clauses. Don't overuse commas!

Tuesday 25th April 2017
OPENING OF MY TEMPTATION STORY.

Additional S.C.- To use sentences of 3 effectively FOR ACTION.
e.g.: Epimetheus opened the door, stepped through the rickety frame and glared straight ahead at the unexpected interruption!

The targets are often written below the cold task; some teachers use a target display board for each child, like the one pictured above from Sandgate Primary in Folkestone, to help both teacher and child know what needs to be focused on. When you look at the hot task at the end of the unit, both the teacher and the child should be able to see progress in the areas identified and reflect both on what has been learned and the next steps that need to be taken to achieve progress.

Adapting your planning in the light of the cold-task assessment

Once the key linguistic focuses of the unit have been identified by the cold task, the teacher writes or adapts the model text, as necessary, to illustrate these key features. Test your model checking that it:

- **has all the language features you want to introduce** at the right level
- **has the language features you want to embed** at the right level to help the children work towards mastery
- **is not too long** (maximum 400 words; 250 is better)
- **is not too detailed**. A good model contains the bare bones of all the features being focused on so they are relatively easy to recognise. The later shared writing provides an opportunity to embellish the model.

See **video clip 5** for an overview of how to plan units of work in Talk for Writing style.

Testing your model

A good way to test your model is to have a go yourself at boxing it up to test its structure (see page 23) and then analyse it and plan what would be the toolkit to accompany the model (see page 25). If your class has been taught in Talk for Writing style before, decide how you will work with the class to add any new features to their already **co-constructed toolkit** for this text type and embed understanding of existing tools. If this is their first time of using the approach, then plan how you are going to co-construct your toolkit of features with the class progressively throughout the unit. Remember that, initially, classes will need lots of help in identifying the tools but, over time, they will grow in confidence and should have the opportunity to identify them themselves; both of these aspects need careful planning.

12 CREATING STORYTELLERS AND WRITERS

Once the unit is underway, a good way of testing whether what you have planned is working is to consider how focused the children are on the work. If you look at the picture here of children working away at improving their writing, you feel that the focus is working.

Chapter 2: Imitation

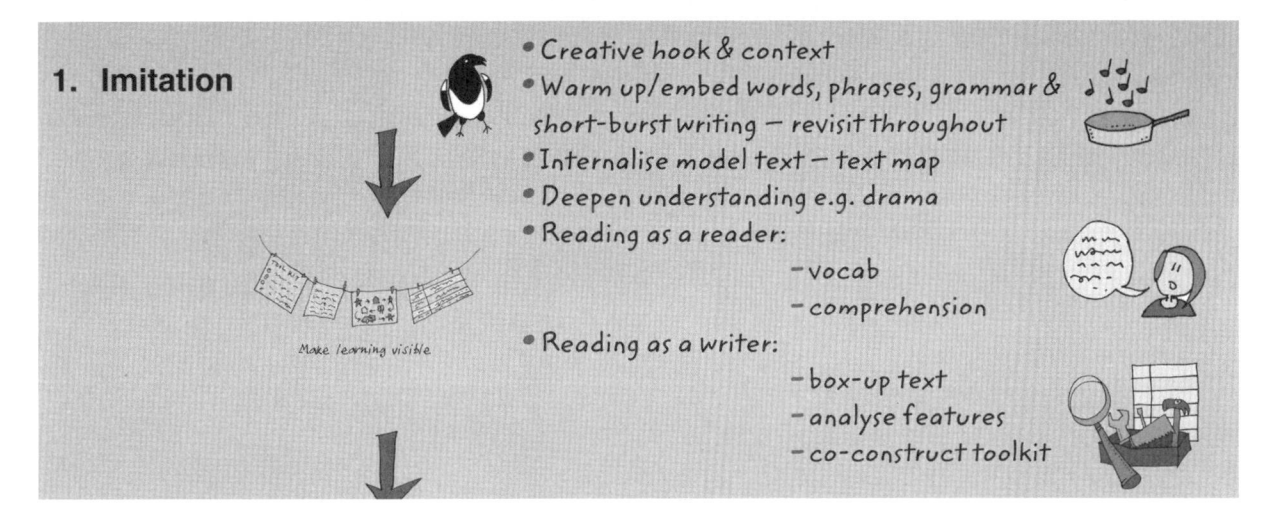

1. Imitation
- Creative hook & context
- Warm up/embed words, phrases, grammar & short-burst writing – revisit throughout
- Internalise model text – text map
- Deepen understanding e.g. drama
- Reading as a reader:
  - vocab
  - comprehension
- Reading as a writer:
  - box-up text
  - analyse features
  - co-construct toolkit

Make learning visible

If the children are unfamiliar with this type of text, then the imitation stage is the most important stage as it lays the pattern of language in the children's heads. If it is rushed, the children will not have internalised the pattern sufficiently to be able to innovate and then use it independently.

The creative hook

Begin the unit with a hook to motivate the children – **see video clip 6**. Amazing sets relating to the topic can be constructed. More simply, the hook could be a filmed message, for example, from someone marooned on an island asking to be rescued, or from the Teaching Assistant (TA) who is explaining how they have been captured by a giant. The children's task would be to write the story of how they escape. The picture shows year 1 teachers at Warren Road Primary, Orpington, dressed as crayons to help get the children involved in writing from a crayon's perspective, based on the story *The Crayons Quit* – watch **video clip 9** to see this in action.

Warming up the words, phrases, sentence patterns and grammar

The assessment of the cold task will have informed the teacher if the children are still not secure in constructing compound or complex sentences, or introducing sentences in a variety of ways. It will enable the teacher to decide what grammar features to integrate into the unit. The sentence patterns of the type of text being focused on, alongside the vocabulary and phrasing that will accompany the context, need to be warmed up at the start of a unit and regularly revisited throughout the unit to help embed these words and phrases. The children need to play around every day with the information and language patterns, interacting with and imitating these patterns as much as possible. The more the text is processed in different ways, the more likely it is that the children will not only understand the text but also internalise the language features.

It is worth the teacher thinking about what the children might find difficult to learn and where there might be challenges in the writing. This will focus attention on what needs to be addressed through language games and activities. This shifts the teaching from becoming a range of entertaining games into focusing upon what needs to be learned in order to help children make progress.

To interact with the text there are, therefore, two strands that need attention:
- mingling with the story content
- interacting with the language patterns.

Look at your model text and decide which words, phrases and grammatical structures will need warming up or embedding so that when the children hear the words and phrases they will know what they mean and how to use them.

To this end, devise a number of games and activities that can be played on a daily basis as 'starters' to warm up and then help embed the tune of the text. These focused games can transform the children's ability to create and write effectively. Think about the key phrasing that underpins the sort of text you want the class to write and what grammar structures are needed. Relevant grammar activities should then be worked out so that the grammar is integrated into the unit and becomes meaningful, as opposed to being the disembodied naming of parts. Activities then need to be devised which will help the children secure understanding of these features. **Video clips 7 & 8** show Pie illustrating some of these activities. The more these activities are oral and engaging, the more chance there is of the children internalising the language that they need for success within the unit.

It is vital that the children understand what the words mean, otherwise imitating a text could just become an exercise in rote learning and hollow chanting. The teacher has to think about how to make sure that the children both understand what they are saying and the pattern in which it is said. Generative grammar cannot work without understanding. It is the underlying principle that underpins 'talking the text'. It is the brain's extraordinary ability to internalise the underlying patterns of language through the constant experience of hearing sentences and then using those patterns to create new utterances. A child who hears and begins to join in with and say a sentence such as, 'Once upon a time, there was a small girl called Amy who ...' will ultimately internalise the pattern as part of their language store, recycling the underlying pattern to create a new statement such as, 'Once there lived, a long, long time ago, a large dinosaur called Dippy who ...'. And, of course, how are you going to help them spell these words?

Video clip 9 shows year 1 teachers in role as crayons warming up the vocabulary that the children will need to write their own letters in role as crayons who want to quit. On this video, you can see that while one teacher teaches the group, the other acts as the teaching assistant and banks all the vocabulary on the flipchart. You might now want to look at **video clip 10** showing a year one pupil from the class, in role as the green crayon, reading her letter about why she wants to quit. Her enthusiasm for what she is saying shows how much she is enjoying her learning and how well she is grasping the meaning of challenging vocabulary.

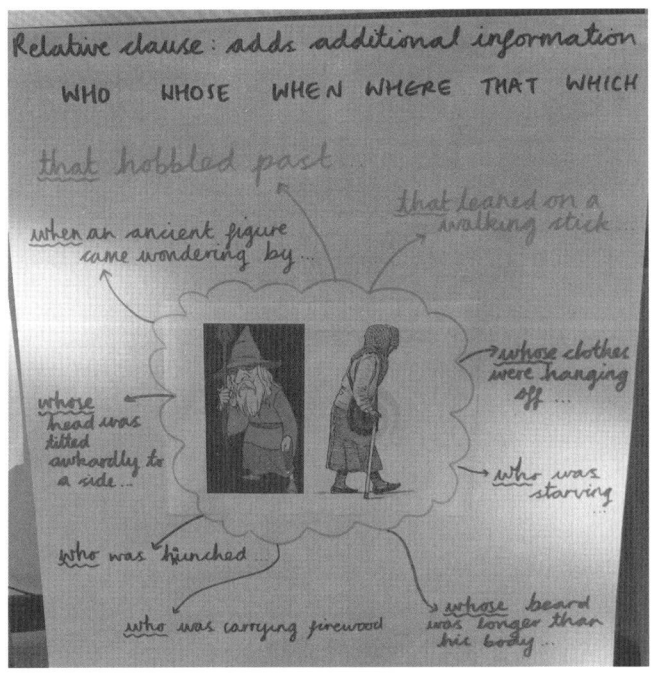

Equally, attention needs to be paid to integrating the grammar needed for a unit into the activities underpinning the unit. The wall display pictured here shows how relative pronouns are used within the text the children are working on. The shared writing would also have contained this feature so that when the children came to write themselves they understood the pattern and purpose of relative pronouns. Such an approach helps children become effective writers – and, if they are in England, disembodied questions about relative pronouns in their SATs test will be water off the proverbial duck's back.

Sentence signposts – the art of linking text

16 CREATING STORYTELLERS AND WRITERS

Sentence signposts are key to making writing coherent. **Video clip 16** explains why teaching key connecting phrases is important and how consistent actions to represent these connectives can help. Time needs to be spent building up children's familiarity with the main sentence signposts. It is, therefore, useful to have a set of actions across the school for signposts like *first*, *after that*, and *finally* and display them both to support the children in using them and to remind the teacher to model their use and extend the range (see **Handout 7** for suggested gestures to illustrate these linking words. Substitute pictures of children for the pictures of Pie, like the example above from St Joseph's, Derby.

Also see **Handout 8**, *The art of linking text*, for an explanation of the different sorts of connecting phrases. Understanding that conjunctions join the parts of sentences together, while fronted adverbials show how a new sentence links to the sentence it follows is key to making writing flow. Integrating grammar into units effectively is particularly important where pupils are faced with challenging grammar tests. For teachers looking for engaging ways to do this, *Jumpstart! Grammar* by Pie and Julia is full of entertaining grammar activities that could easily be adapted to fit the topic of any unit. As the quotation below emphasises, well chosen random association games can fire children's imagination and bring our their creativity:

> *When Pie Corbett came to teach us, I didn't think that it would help by just throwing in random ideas. However, as he went along, I realised it allowed us to become more creative. This has helped my writing because I now think about every word I use and the effect it would have on the reader.*
> – Dujour, aged 9, St George's Primary, Battersea, London

The picture here shows children from Sandgate Primary in Folkestone sorting main and subordinate clauses in sentences in preparation for using such structures in their writing. It is the assessment influencing the teaching that sharpens and clarifies the learning experiences. And, of course, many of these activities will lead to short-burst writing activities, thus ensuring some creative writing is done every day even when the focus is on internalising text orally.

A note on short-burst writing: short-burst writing is a brilliant way of warming up all the key writing techniques that help hook and keep a reader engaged. It can be integrated into all units. How to do short-burst writing is the focus of a separate Talk for Writing booklet and DVD (due to be published in 2018).

To help children internalise the language patterns of a unit you might:

- Rehearse specific spelling patterns that will be needed for this writing
- Put sentence signposts (words and phrases that help link text and tell the reader the direction in which the text is heading) and other key language features onto cards and rehearse them
- Play 'linking phrase of the day' where you all have to try and slip the sentence signpost into classroom conversation and activity (*because … whereas … At that moment … It was not until … Without hesitating …* etc.)
- Take a pattern such as an adverb starter (*Amazingly, Usefully, Incredibly, Weirdly, Helpfully*) and challenge the children to see who can 'use' that construction during the day
- Try sentence games where you change bland language, extend sentences, alter sentence openings, drop in or add on information, trim back wordy sentences as well as 'sentence doctor' errors
- Play rapid sentence games where you write up a key pattern and then children have to invent sentences using the same pattern. Imitate sentences orally first and then in writing (using mini whiteboards), e.g.
    - They looked up quickly when the door opened.
    - They watched in silence when the boat left the shore.
    - When the door opened, they looked up quickly.
    - When the boat left the shore, they watched in silence.

When playing the drama games suggested above, make sure that children use 'fiction' language. You could even give a simple score for the correct use of different features.

To help children understand the context, among other things, you might:

- Interview a child in role as 'The Great Narrator – the world expert on storytelling – who will describe the setting of say a haunted castle in their own words, then ask all the children to have a go in pairs
- Hold 'back to back' mobile phone conversations about the story
- Interview different characters from the story
- Model how to present the story as a news broadcast
- Hot seat characters from the story
- Act out scenes
- Retell the story from a different character's perspective.

18 CREATING STORYTELLERS AND WRITERS

Internalising the model text

> *Dear Pie Corbett,*
> *I am writing to you because I think your ideas about how to get children to stand up and say stories is brilliant. I used to hate writing. It was boring listening to the teacher groan on and on because I would just sit there and do nothing. Also, then it was hard. Now I love it because it is so much more easy and I produce more work. I think it's got easier because our teacher teaches us all the things and then we learn stories that include all the things. I also feel more confident ...*
> – Pupil's letter presented as evidence of impact by teacher from Sheffield

Internalising the pattern of language of the model text by learning it orally, lies at the heart of the Talk for Writing approach – see **video clip 11** for an example of how to do this. The younger the class, the more time needs to be spent on helping the children internalise the pattern of the language. The picture here shows a nursery class at St George's, Battersea, internalising *The Gingerbread Man*. The teacher speaks the text in a lively manner and the children join in with both the speaking of the language and the actions that make it memorable and creative. The children do not see the text at this stage but there is a simple text map of images or key events to act as a reminder plus actions to reinforce specific language patterns as well as the meaning.

The class works on internalising the text over a number of days until it begins to become second nature, with the teacher increasingly handing over to the class. It is crucial for the patterns to be 'over-learned' if they are to actually become part of the child's linguistic repertoire. **Video clip 14** explains why internalising text is so important. As the text becomes embedded in the children's memories, the teacher moves from whole-class imitation to group performances down to trios and pairs. Pairs sit facing each other with the text maps or mini washing lines between them – saying the text at the same time like a mirror, using actions. There are many ways to vary the learning of a text, e.g.

- Say it in pairs like a mirror
- Pass it round the circle
- Perform it like a tennis match – word for word, chunk for chunk or sentence by sentence, back and forth
- Mime it
- Say it as fast as possible – babble gabble – racing to see who can get to the end first

IMITATION

- Pass it up and down a line
- Present the text as a group, using a PowerPoint or other forms of illustration.

As children grow older, more sophisticated ways can be found of internalising text. Once they are familiar with a particular pattern of language, they will be able to hear a story and immediately be able to retell it embellishing it as they go. The picture here shows a year 6 class at St Joseph's, Derby, working as a group to embellish a model text.

Many schools build in regular opportunities for children to talk their text, presenting the information to other classes and even performing in assemblies. The provision of audience and purpose is always a spur to learning, refining and honing the use of language.

The initial stage of 'talking the text' mirrors the stage where children learn to retell a known tale. Where children are unfamiliar with a text type or struggle with literacy, it is worth spending time helping the children internalise the basic patterns of the text – in the long run, this pays off because you will see the patterns reappearing in their own writing. This is rather like putting a writing frame into the children's minds in a memorable, meaningful manner.

A note on drawing text maps

Draw a text map that sums up the overall flow of the text. It's important to keep the map and the drawings simple, as fussy, over-detailed maps with an image for every word are much harder to 'read'. Soon the children will be drawing their own version. (The story text map here, from Yew Tree Community Primary in Birmingham, is ideal. The simple pictures mean that you can immediately start to "read" it. The teacher is focusing on connecting phrases and so these words are in writing rather than being represented by icons.) If you are artistic, try to make your map simple – the idea is that they can be drawn quickly by anyone as an aide memoire: the more artistic a map, the more daunted children will be when drawing their own maps. **Video clip 15** shows how to text map a story and help the children tell the it expressively.

Top tips for imitating the text

You may find the following tips useful in helping you teach children how to imitate text. Also look at **video clip 12** to see how Pie does it. **Video clip 13** shows two children from different schools demonstrating how powerful the approach can be and **clip 14** explains why internalising text is so important.

- Make certain you and your teaching assistant have over-learnt the model text very well so that you can lead the storytelling with gusto.
- Draw a simple text map; do not have an icon for every word.
- Devise a few actions that will help everyone remember the key language patterns and content. The children will enjoy joining in with this and suggesting better actions. Avoid too many actions.
- Once the preparations are in place, immerse the children thoroughly in the model text. Remember, you are the model so say the words clearly, with expression, and make the movements with energy so everyone can enjoy joining in. Keep looking at the text map to support you and the class: this is not a memory test.
- Get the children to sketch their own text map as this will help imprint the text in their heads. Outlaw clip art – not only does this waste hours of time but it also breaks the connection between hand and brain.
- Finally, remember to focus on getting the children to intonate the text properly and remember, if they sound dull, that's because you sounded dull. Increasingly, hand over to the children so they can talk the text independently with enthusiasm.

A note on punctuation: Some teachers like to get the children to voice the punctuation of the text so the children may say something like this: *George (open brackets) a particularly noisy child (close brackets)* ... Inserting words to represent all the punctuation removes the meaning from the text and makes it sound very strange. The whole point of imitating text is to embed the pattern of language. Therefore, the children need to hear the pattern of the language in a meaningful way. Expression helps children 'hear' the punctuation. To help them remember the punctuation, it can be useful to use actions instead, like punching the air for full stops, or stamping out the stop. Hand movements to indicate commas, for example, for dropped in information, are particularly useful.

Once the children have internalised the text, there are two key steps that help bridge the move from imitation to innovation: A. Reading as a reader and B. Reading as a writer, which includes co-constructing the toolkit for the type of text focused on.

A) Reading as a reader

Once the children have internalised the text, they will need to see what the text looks like in written form. The longer this moment can be delayed, the more likely the children are to have internalised the patterns. **Video clip 18** explains how to introduce the written version of the text. If the children know the text intimately, then it will mean that even those who struggle with reading have access to the written version, as they already know what it is going to say. This removes the barrier that reading problems can produce when studying a text and helps the child become a reader since prior knowledge is key to deciphering text meaningfully.

Below is a simple model text for introducing how to write a journey story. The key sentence signposts have been highlighted to help the children see the importance of these. 'Reading as a reader' aids comprehension. To support understanding with young children all the relevant props would need to be available, like a model cat, and a duck alongside images of clock towers etc plus a bag with the appropriate food in it.

Little Charlie

Once upon a time, there was a little boy called Charlie **who** lived in a big, big city. **One day, when** he woke up, his mother said to him, "Take this bag to your grandmother's." **Into the bag**, she put a slice of cheese, a loaf of bread and a square of chocolate.

Next, he walked and he walked and he walked **until** he came to a bridge. Miaouw!!! There was a cat – a lean cat, a mean cat.

"I'm hungry," said the cat. "What have you got in your bag?"

Charlie replied that he had a slice of cheese, a loaf of bread – **but** he kept the chocolate hidden!

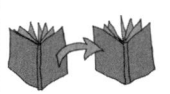

"I'll have the cheese please," said the cat and ate it all up.

Next, he walked and he walked and he walked until he came to a pond. There he met a duck – a lovely black and white duck.

"I'm hungry," said the duck. "What have you got in your bag?"

Charlie replied that he had a loaf of bread – **but** he kept the chocolate hidden!

"I'll have the bread please," said the duck and it ate it all up.

Next, he walked and he walked and he walked until he came to a tall town clock – tick tock, tick tock, tick tock. There he met not one, not two **but** three, scruffy pigeons.

"We're hungry," said the pigeons. "What have you got in your bag?"

Unfortunately, there was only the chocolate! **Luckily**, Charlie found some crumbs **so** he scattered them on the ground and the pigeons ate them all up.

Next, he walked and he walked and he walked until he came to a crossroads. There he met …. Nobody. "Mmmm, I'm hungry ," said Charlie.

"What have I got in my bag? Mmmmmm, chocolate!" **So**, he ate it all up!

Next, he walked and he walked and he walked until he came to Grandma's house. There he met Grandma.

"I'm hungry," said Grandma. "What have you got in your bag?"

Unfortunately, there was only the chocolate wrapper. **Luckily**, grandma had made pizza and chips for tea. *Retelling © Pie Corbett*

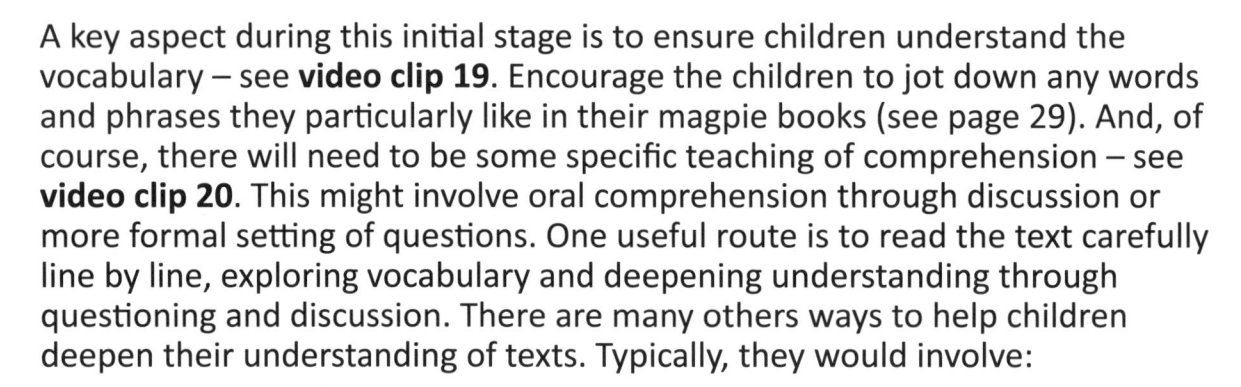

A key aspect during this initial stage is to ensure children understand the vocabulary – see **video clip 19**. Encourage the children to jot down any words and phrases they particularly like in their magpie books (see page 29). And, of course, there will need to be some specific teaching of comprehension – see **video clip 20**. This might involve oral comprehension through discussion or more formal setting of questions. One useful route is to read the text carefully line by line, exploring vocabulary and deepening understanding through questioning and discussion. There are many others ways to help children deepen their understanding of texts. Typically, they would involve:

- Talking about the text (oral comprehension). An excellent book explaining how to open up discussion on text so that the children co-construct understanding rather than trying to work out the answer they think you want to hear, is Aidan Chambers *Tell me*, published by Thimble Press, which explains the underpinning techniques of what is sometimes referred to as booktalk – see **video clip 21**
- Acting the text out
- Hot seating characters
- Filling gaps – cloze procedure – taking out key language features such as linking words or phrases
- Comparing sentences and discussing which is most effective and why
- Sequencing – splitting up sentences, paragraphs or even whole texts for children to re-assemble – this helps confirm the organisation of language
- Improving – provide weak sentences or paragraphs and the children have to 'improve' them
- Focused vocabulary work relating to the passage
- Shared reading of the model together paying particular attention to the punctuation
- Finding other examples to read to broader the frame of reference.

Video clip 22 is a very useful overview of reading-as-a-reader strategies. If you are interested in finding out more about how you can develop powerful readers in your school, see the Booklet and DVD *Talk for Reading*, based on a very successful conference presented by Pie Corbett. It includes all the DVD school footage presented at that conference (available Spring 2018).

B) Reading as a writer

To lead into the next phase of innovation, the children must first be involved in analysing the text that they have internalised. There are two key aspects that the teacher has to ensure happen:
- pupils understand the underlying structure of the text through the simple device of boxing up
- pupils recognise and understand the features that helped to make the writing effective by helping to co-construct a toolkit of ingredients.

i) Boxing up the structure of text

First, show the children how to box up the text. This involves the children in using a problem-solving approach to see if they can identify how the text is organised and boxing it up into a grid which forms a template for the structure of that sort of text. Boxing up has proved to be a simple yet very powerful way of helping pupils first understand the structure of a text and then to use a similar structure to plan a similar text of their own. Create a two-column grid with as many rows as there are paragraphs/sections in the text as illustrated in **video clip 23**. Then involve the class in identifying what the heading would be for each section. In non-fiction text this is often easier than in fiction text as there may be headings or obvious topic sentences that clearly indicate the subject matter found in each section. With fiction, help the class to see the underpinning plot. For example, a simple tale like Little Miss Muffet has an underlying plot that has been used many thousands of times, as illustrated below:

Boxing up the structure of Miss Muffet

Underlying structure (heading for each section)	Key events in particular story
Main character (MC) in cosy setting	Miss M sitting & eating happily
Enter the threat	Spider enters
MC escapes	Miss M runs scared

This illustrates the simple story structure of a beginning a middle and an end. Carry out the boxing up with the children so that that the class co-constructs their understanding of the structure. Where children are working on a text type for the first time, working out the basic underlying pattern as a class is very handy as it leads the children into writing something similar with a predetermined structure.

The first example here, from Montgomery Primary in Birmingham, shows how boxing up can be adapted to suit young children. The first column in the grid shows the

24 CREATING STORYTELLERS AND WRITERS

classic story structure of an opening, followed by the build up, the problem, the resolution and concluded by the ending. The key details of the story have then been entered into the second column in pictorial text map form. As children get older, boxing up becomes more sophisticated but it is probably a good idea to maintain the simple essence of boxing up so that children can clearly see the underpinning structure of the model. This then acts as the underpinning structure when they come to innovate on the model and plan and write their own version – see pages 33–35.

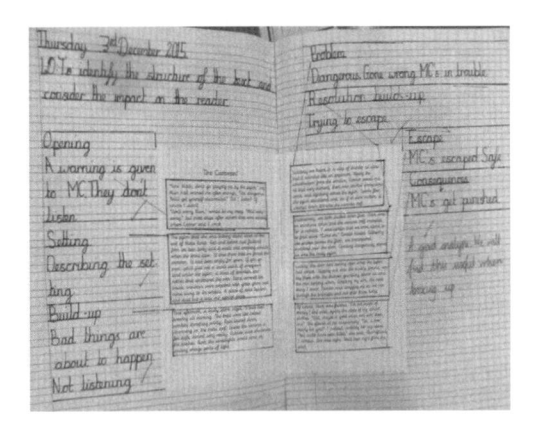

Once children have been shown how to box up text, it is very important to get them to do the boxing up themselves, so they really start to understand how different types of stories are structured. For example, Knowle Park Primary, Bristol, uses *The Caravan* as the model text for a warning story. As the child's book here shows, the pupils have then boxed up and annotated the text themselves to show how it has been structured.

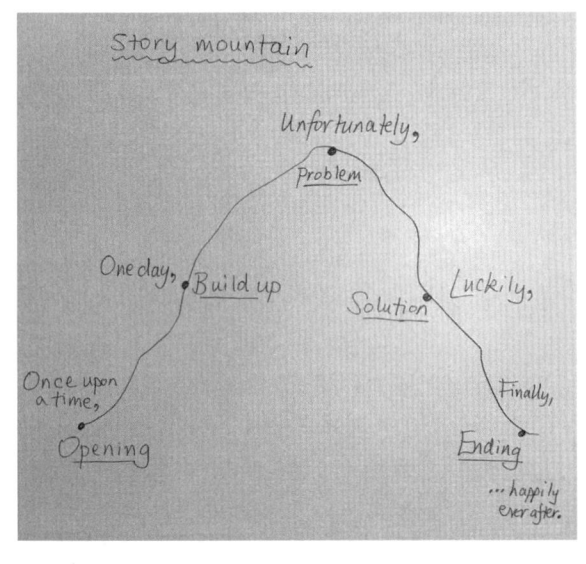

In nursery, reception and year one, many teachers use the simple story-mountain planner to plan basic stories. As illustrated here, these help children visualise the key sentence signposts that introduce the different stages of the story and round it off. By year 2, moving over to boxing up is recommended as this allows for a much greater range of planning. Story mountains suit simple substitution and addition; boxing up, if taught correctly through involving the children in analysing how a text has been ordered, builds understanding of structure and helps lead to creative independent structuring. **Handouts 5a & 5b** show how the underlying pattern of 8 key story types can be boxed up alongside building in progression for older children.

It is important to co-construct the boxing up with the class and ensure that the children increasingly become able to box up text for themselves and then use a similar pattern to box up their own version. This enables them to think for themselves about the audience and purpose of their writing, and then construct their own boxed-up grids deciding what sections they want to include and in what order they should come.

You can adapt the boxing up approach to support understanding of any text. Many longer paragraphs have a beginning, a middle and an end, just like a longer text has; equally, the structure of a novel can be boxed up by looking at the overall structure of chapters to show how the whole story has been shaped. Boxing up is both simple and extremely powerful as this teacher explains:

> *Boxing up works across all text types and genres. Making this a key component for all text analysis and planning for writing helped children feel control of learning as each text type could be dealt with in the same way.*
> – Teacher from Lewisham Talk for Writing project

It's worth remembering that the boxed-up structure for each type of non-fiction text is easier to grasp than those for key story types like portal stories or defeating the monster because the underpinning structure tends to be more consistent and it is easier for the children to see the pattern. Time needs to be spent early on helping children grasp these underpinning story patterns – then they will much more easily be able to plan a story for themselves. More confident writers should also look at other examples of the same genre to broaden their frame of reference.

Co-constructing the toolkit

Once the children have understood how the text is structured, they will benefit from using a problem-solving approach to identifying key language features that might be useful for 'when we write our own one'. This is rather like 'raiding the reading' or magpieing – stealing good ideas. Use a range of methods to help them analyse all the ingredients that contribute to making the text effective. Underlining and highlighting are useful techniques as children search for the basic ingredients of the text type like linking phrases (sentence signposts) or powerful descriptive phrases. This becomes easier if they look at how several writers have tackled a type of writing, for they can generalise the sorts of patterns that typically appear.

Once a new feature has been identified, get the children to explain what they have just learnt and add the feature to your toolkit of ingredients for this particular type of text; examples can be displayed on the washing line to support understanding. In this manner, a toolkit for each text type can be co-constructed with the children listing the ingredients to choose from to make this sort of writing effective.

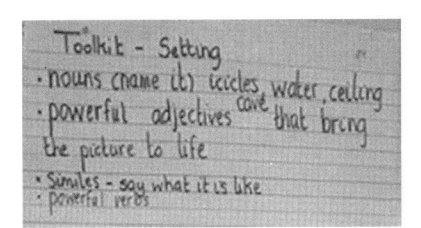

The first example here is a setting toolkit that has been co-constructed with a reception class at St Matthew's, Birmingham, who were doing short-burst writing. The second example, at the top of the next page, shows how the mind-mapping approach can be used to draw out the ingredients that help to create engaging characters. Toolkits in reception and year 1 are sometimes called Writing Secrets and are often very visual. As the children grow older, these toolkits are further developed so that the features are added to year on year. **Appendix 2** illustrates how the development of the underpinning toolkits for the 6 key features underpinning fiction writing (settings, suspense, characterisation, dialogue, description, and openings and endings) need to be co-constructed progressively with classes so that they increasingly internalise the features and start to select the ingredients they want automatically.

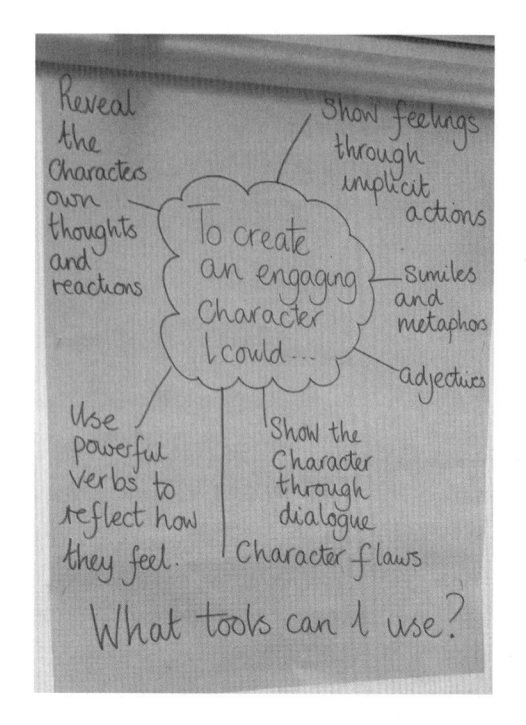

Different teachers have chosen different visual ways of developing this idea to suit the needs of their classes. The example here from Hallsville Primary shows how the model text, after it has been internalised and then analysed, can be annotated in front of the class to become the toolkit of tools not rules for writing this sort of text. The most important thing is that the toolkit is co-constructed with the class in child-friendly language so that it is meaningful and therefore useful. At the bottom of the picture, you can see that the teacher is reminding the children to remember what effect the features have on the reader. Talk for Writing is all about helping children to become effective readers as well as writers.

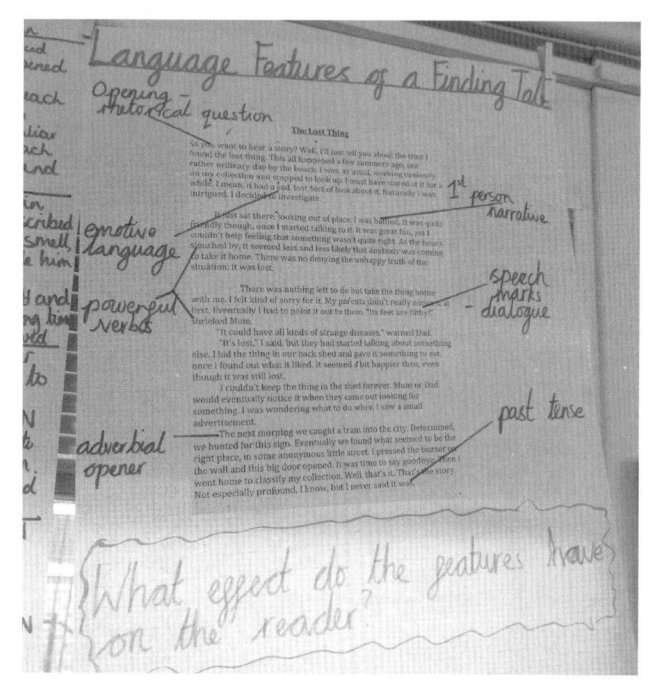

The next example, is a suspense toolkit. The use of icons to represent each tool is an excellent way of helping pupils recall the features. The use of colour coding also helps to distinguish the examples from the features they exemplify.

Beware of disembodied tick lists of features or strange grammatical terms

Co-constructing toolkits is much more effective than listing a series of success criteria and sticking them in the children's books. These lists are often meaningless for the children because they have not understood what the features mean – see **video clip 24**. If they are involved in co-constructing the lists and, if the toolkits include examples of what the features mean, and they have played warm-up games to get used to the features and been shown how to use them in shared writing, then they will support the children's learning. In England, with the rise and rise of the grammar tests, there is a tendency for teachers to just list disembodied grammar features in their toolkits. If you were asked to write a powerful description of a person that you know and care about and were given the following features to include:

- adjectives
- fronted adverbials
- the subjunctive mood
- semi-colons
- the past progressive

you would not find the list helpful; neither do the children. If the list had been co-constructed with meaningful features for this type of text supported by useful examples, then it could help. Moreover, if your list is just a list of grammar features, it would probably relate to most types of writing so it is doubly useless.

For older children, it's a good idea to express the writerly feature in child-friendly language and give an example (preferably in a different colour). If you want to bring out particular grammatical aspects, annotate these in another colour. For example:

Select powerful **verbs** to help the reader picture the scene:
*e.g. She would **whizz** through the waves.*

Practical toolkits can also be created that are, literally, boxes of the key language features needed for the text being focused on. Many of the warming-up and embedding activities from the unit can be found in the box and the children can refer to them for support. The picture here from Warren Road Primary, Orpington, shows children working on suspense text so the toolkit box includes work on empty words, on words and phrases to build tension, and sentences of three to slow down the action.

Everyday toolkits

Many schools have also developed what might be called *Everyday, Always or All the time toolkits*. These are features like writing in sentences that begin with a capital letter and end with a full stop. Such features always apply whatever text

28 CREATING STORYTELLERS AND WRITERS

is being focused on. The examples pictured belows are from Maidwell Primary in Northampton where years one and two are taught together. The picture enables us to see how these *All the time toolkits* can be built on year by year to ensure progress is planned into units of work. In this way, the children are aware of the underpinning features that must always be present in their writing and that they must check for carefully when reading their writing through.

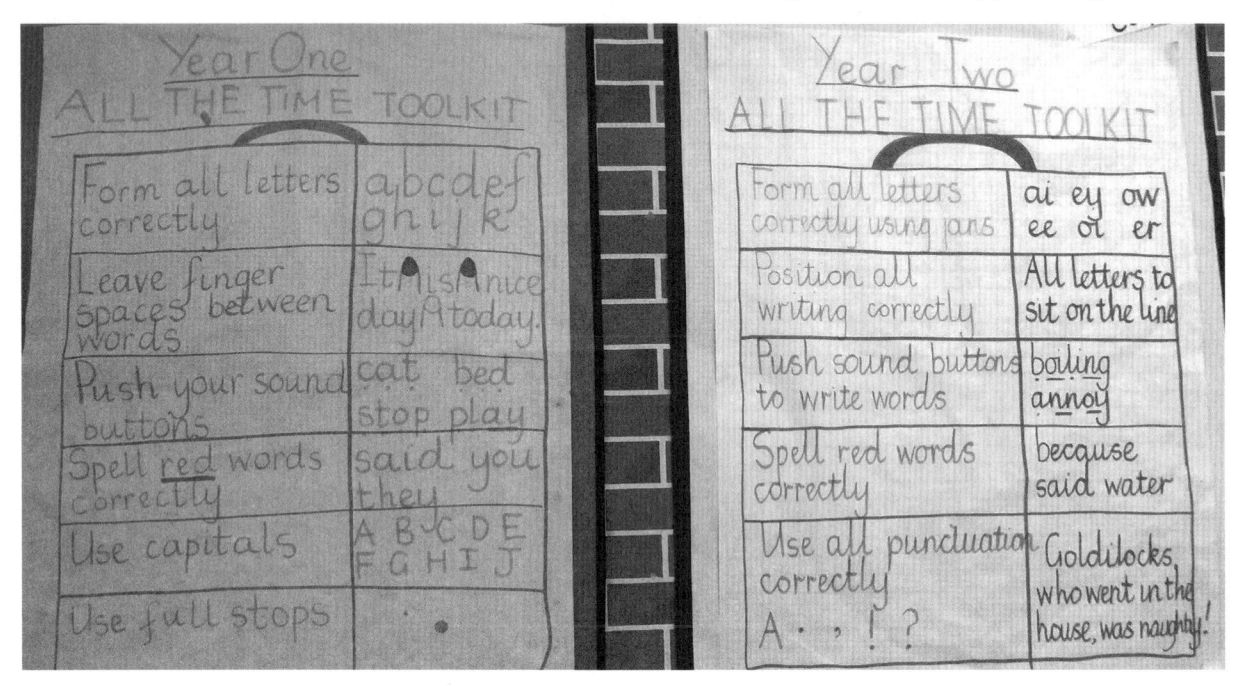

It may also help if older children are introduced to the fact that there are basically four things that you have to do to try to ensure that any piece of writing works (plan it, link it, express it, check it). By year 5, the everyday toolkit may look like this:

The everyday toolkit for success for any writing

Plan it	• Remember audience and purpose – you have to engage and interest your reader • Box up your ideas including a beginning with a hook
Link it	• Link your ideas, with good sentence signposts • Use topic sentences to orientate your reader. • Read it aloud to check that it flows
Express it	• Use a range of sentence types and structures • Select which hook-your-reader tools you want to use to keep your reader engaged • Select just the right words to say what you want to say
Check it	• Read it aloud and see if it sounds good – does it hold your interest? • Does it say what you wanted it to say effectively? • Is it paragraphed clearly? • Is your spelling and punctuation correct?

These generic ingredients could then become part of the children's inner toolkit around which they can build the specific features relating to the type of writing focused on.

Display the toolkits on the washing line or working wall so they support the children when they start to write and encourage them to jot down key features and favourite words in their magpie books/writing journals.

What is a magpie book?

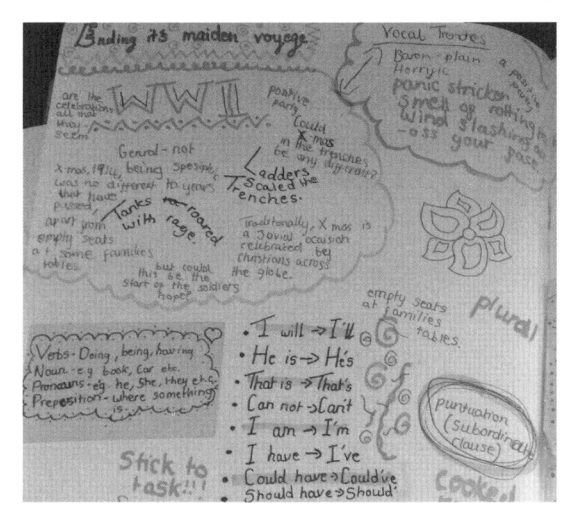

Magpie books, sometimes known as writing journals, act as a 'writing thesaurus'. Into this, the children can stick the model text, the boxed-up structure to show the organisation, the writing toolkit of ingredients plus useful banks of words, sentence patterns, tips, hints and reminders of different story patterns. This could include notes on fiction, poetry and non-fiction text types. The magpie book acts as a reminder or reference point when children are writing and encourages them to reflect on their learning and savour language. Children enjoy noting down things to remember or use when writing, as illustrated above from St Joseph's Primary in Derby. Most importantly, these magpie books are personal: you can see from this page from a child's writing journal from East Hunsbury School in Northampton that the child is enjoying noting things down in a way that suits them. For this reason, it is a good idea to resist the temptation to control how the children organise their magpie books but rather leave the organisation up to each individual child.

Typically, children will be noticing the use of features like these:
- sentence signposts that help to steer the reader through the text – *because, Just at that moment, In the distance ...*
- generalising words that help the writer to sum up things – *most, usually, the majority of, ...*
- persuasive devices such as 'boastful adjectives' – *magnificent, impressive ...*
- 'bossy' verbs (imperatives) that allow a writer to push the reader to a viewpoint or instruct the reader – *Imagine ...Listen ... Picture how ...*

30 CREATING STORYTELLERS AND WRITERS

Making the learning visible

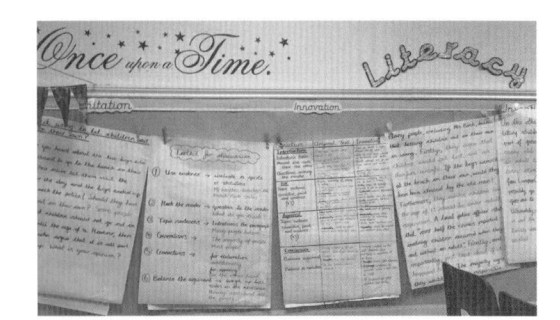

By the end of the imitation stage, all of the learning that the children have experienced in the unit so far should be visible on the learning wall or washing line – see **video clip 25**. The picture here shows a working wall at Knowle Park, Bristol. The teacher has chosen to display the information like a washing line to underline the logical order of the information displayed. The children should be able to see the model text, the boxed-up plan, the co-constructed toolkit and any word or phrase banks that have been created to help them with their learning. It also, of course, helps the teacher and the teaching assistant to remain focused on the key learning targets.

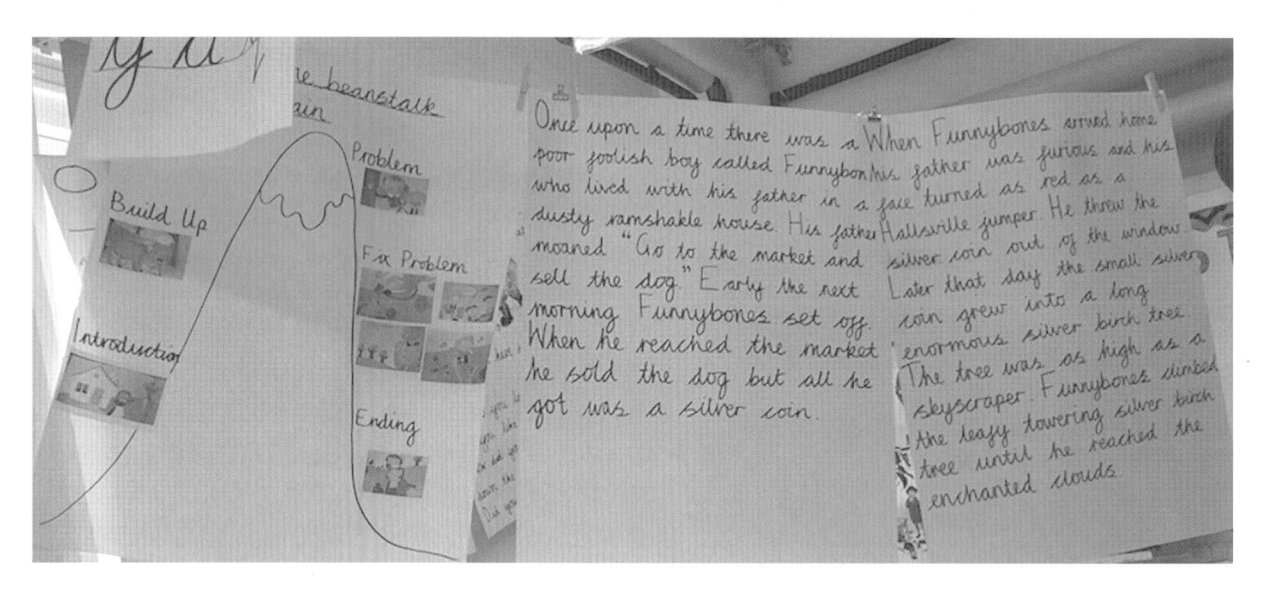

This section of a washing line display pictured above, shows the story mountain (used with younger classes instead of boxing up) plus the model text.

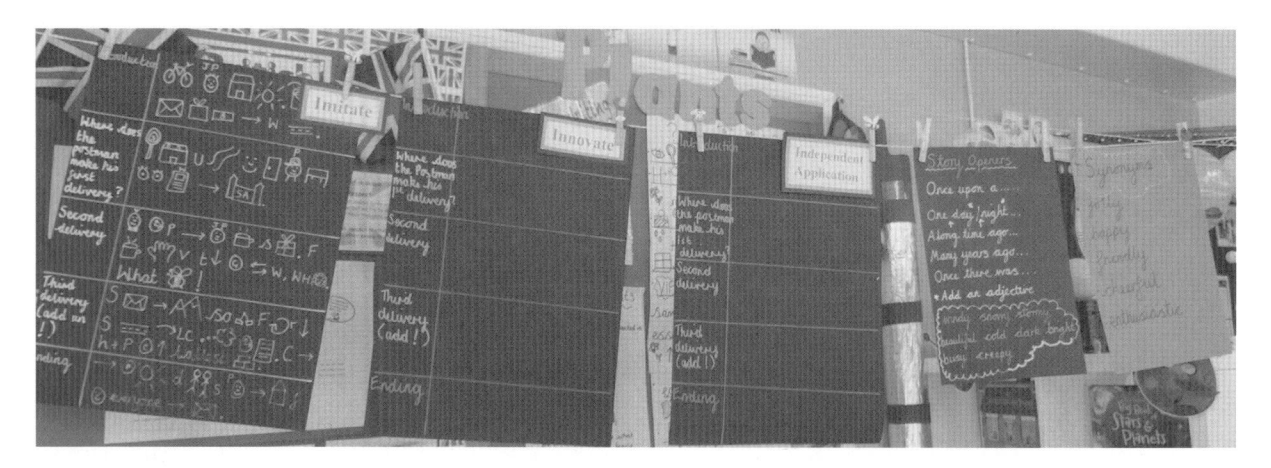

The washing line above is from Selby Community Primary, Yorkshire. By using black flipchart paper, the text is highly visible (like traditional blackboards). This washing line is being built up throughout the unit so that the stages of the learning process are highly visible. The children will have been involved in boxing up the model at the end of the imitation stage. When the innovation stage is reached they will be involved in boxing up the innovated version as a class and then boxing up their own innovation. Finally, in the independent application stage, they will use boxing up to plan their independent work. And, of course, at the end of the unit, it is important to display the quality of the work achieved, as illustrated here by a display of work on *The Papaya that Spoke* from West St Leonard's Primary School.

Working in partnership with your TA to make learning visible

The approach works best when the teacher and the teaching assistant (TA) work in partnership actively supporting the children's learning. The picture here from Hallsville Primary School, Newham, shows the dual approach in action. The teacher is developing the text with the class while the TA is scribing the sentences as they are decided. This approach is illustrated on **video clip 9** and also by Julia working as Pie's TA in many of the clips. While one is teaching, the

32 CREATING STORYTELLERS AND WRITERS

other can be visually drawing out the key learning points for the children by, for example:

- Magpieing useful words and phrases onto flipcharts
- Drawing text maps in response to the pupils' ideas
- Listing the key ingredients for toolkits as they arise out of discussion with pupils
- Boxing up the text in response to pupil input
- Adding ideas to flipcharts.

All of these resources can then be used as posters on the writing wall or washing line supporting the children's writing. If the resources are created in front of the children and are co-constructed out of their discussions, they will be meaningful.

In many Talk for Writing schools, if there isn't a teaching assistant, the children are trained to take on that difficult role because acting as the TA really helps pupils to focus on their learning. To the left, you can see a girl from Montgomery Primary in Birmingham noting down the descriptive phrases arising from a class discussion; shortly afterwards, a boy took her place.

Performing the text

By the end of the imitation stage, the children should be very familiar with the overall pattern of the model they have internalised and its various language features – they will have heard, spoken, read, discussed and played with the sentence types till they have begun to become part of their linguistic repertoire. It would be ideal to end this stage with some sort of enthusiastic performance to other classes as in the picture here from Front Lawn Academy, Havant, where year 5 were performing for another class. With younger classes, invite the parents in at the end of the day and get them to join in. The language patterns can then be further embedded at home and all the family can have fun. For detailed information of how to do this, see *Talk for Writing in the Early Years*.

Chapter 3: Innovation

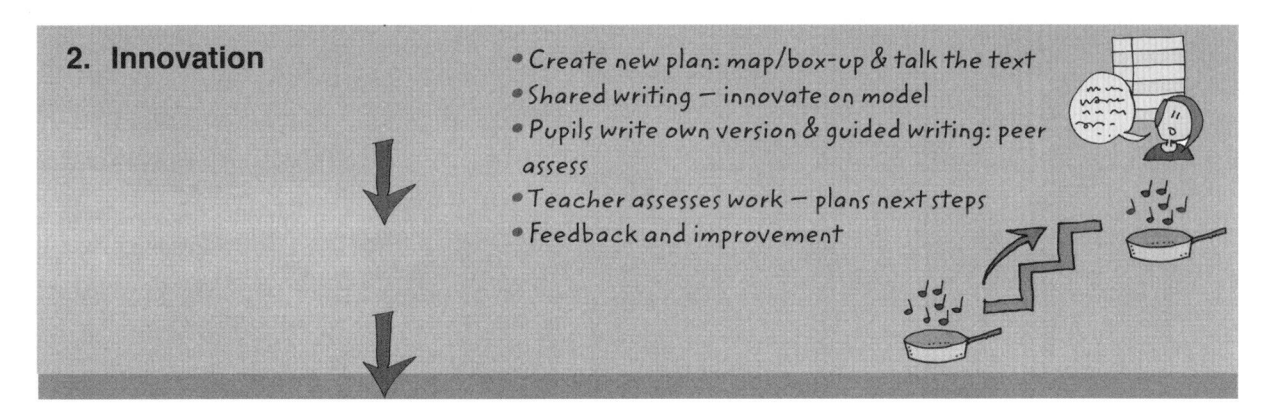

2. Innovation
- Create new plan: map/box-up & talk the text
- Shared writing — innovate on model
- Pupils write own version & guided writing: peer assess
- Teacher assesses work — plans next steps
- Feedback and improvement

Once the children have become familiar with the original text, they are ready to move into the second phase, which involves using the original as a basis for creating something new – so that they can write their own version. Do not move on to innovation until the original model is deeply embedded as you cannot innovate on something that is only vaguely known.

Shared planning: boxing up the plan for the innovation

The teacher will now need to plan a new engaging starting point and setting for the innovated version, as a basis for the children's writing since all of us write best about what we know about – and what matters to us.

By this point, the original model will be displayed, with the text boxed up and annotated – accompanied by lists of the key ingredients as well as writing reminders, techniques and tricks which have all been drawn out of discussions with the children. These should be on the washing line or working wall so that the teacher can refer to them, as well as being inside the children's magpie books/writing journals for their own personal reference.

The boxed-up grid from the original model can be used as a basic planner – see **video clip 27**. New information needs to be gathered and organised onto the grid. With fiction, this is relatively easy as the children can imaginatively contribute to crafting the under-pinning features of the innovated story. The great thing about boxing up is that it not only allows you to analyse the model text but you can then add in additional columns and use the same structure to plan your innovation on the model. The children can then add another column and plan their innovation.

34 CREATING STORYTELLERS AND WRITERS

If you look at the picture above of a boy at Yew Tree Community School, Birmingham, writing a warning story, you can see that he is using his boxed-up planning to help write his innovation.

The idea is that the children draw upon the underlying structure and language features of the original model, to enable them to create their own version about a different topic. To put it simply, the children might have already spent a week learning about the underpinning structure of journey stories through learning orally a basic journey text like *Little Charlie*. This is then used as a basis for writing a new text about Little Elif. The picture here from Hallsville shows the generic boxed-up plan in the middle. To the left of the grid is the analysis showing how the structure relates to the model text. The text to the right shows how the structure is being used to plan the innovated text.

As explained earlier, with younger classes a story mountain will often be used rather than boxing up to help children plan their stories, moving from setting the scene, to the coming of a problem, to the resolution of the problem and the ending. The picture here from Yew Tree Community School in Birmingham shows two boys working on their story mountain so they can innovate on the class model.

Another good way of helping young children to understand how they can innovate simply on a given pattern, illustrated by **video clip 26**, is to use the story text map plus Post-it notes (at least it's good as long as the Post-it notes don't fall off). Children can then visually see how the changes have been made, as illustrated by this picture from Hallsville showing how the opening two sections of a story have been innovated. **But beware, this method should be moved away from by the end of KS1 because it encourages the children to hug very closely to the original model.**

Depending on the children's needs, it can be useful to draw a new text map or washing line and to 'talk the new text' in pairs, refining ideas and trying out different ways of expressing ideas, views and information. Refer back to the original to check for useful language features that might be recycled. Pairs can come to the front and present their text orally, receiving feedback from the teacher and class. This acts as a model so that pairs feedback to other pairs, working as response partners, identifying where an oral text works effectively as well as making suggestions for improvement. It can also be beneficial for children to practise retelling their innovated version on their own. The picture here shows a girl from St Joseph's in Derby doing just that. As you can see, she is concentrating on her text map for her innovation and running through what she wants to say in her head.

During innovation, it is important to keep playing spelling and sentence games so that the children have plenty of oral and written practice in the language features that they will need when they come to write. It can also be handy to play drama games to develop a text further with creative activities such as hot seating characters or interviewing bystanders. These tune the children in to the language they will need to use. One simple game is to work in pairs and use the phrase, 'Tell me more about ...' to encourage the children to develop and extend ideas prior to writing.

Shared writing – innovating on the model

The teacher then uses the boxed-up plan to move from an oral version into writing. During shared writing with the class, the text will be further refined, often referring back to the original model or models. It is important for the teacher to involve the children in the composition, taking suggestions and pushing the children to refine their ideas so that they are fluent, coherent and effective. The picture here shows shared writing in action with a year 5 class at Selby Community Primary. To maximise pupil involvement, the teacher gets all the children on the carpet and uses a whiteboard to scribe the text at their eye level. At all times, the teacher needs to bear in mind the level that the text should be written at – which should be above the standard of the children. To put it simply, if the children are writing at what teachers in England all used to understand as level 2 then the class composition must be at level 3.

Of course, life is never this simple and there are no classes where children are all writing at the same level. This is why teachers use guided writing to group children according to their need and to teach them at their level. Many teachers find it useful to develop a text over several days, focusing on different aspects. Key points need to be referred to and included so that the shared writing is an opportunity to teach progress. During shared writing, the teacher or the children may explain why one idea is more effective than another. The teacher pushes the children to generate possibilities and to judge what would work best. Everyone should be drawing on the original model, as well as the list of ingredients while being driven by using their writing techniques to make the composition powerful. See **video clip 29** as an example of this. **Handout 9** may also be useful here as it lists the sort of phrases you use to involve the children in shared writing. One very useful tip when composing is to model for the children how to **use a dotted line under any words that they find hard**. This has two important effects. First, it illustrates that when composing it is not a good idea to break your flow and start looking words up in a dictionary. Keep writing and check the spelling later. Secondly, it shows that they must never 'dodge' a good word they wish to use because they can't spell it. This is also very useful for the teacher, the TA and any child in role as TA at the flip chart when children suggest words that they may have difficulty in spelling.

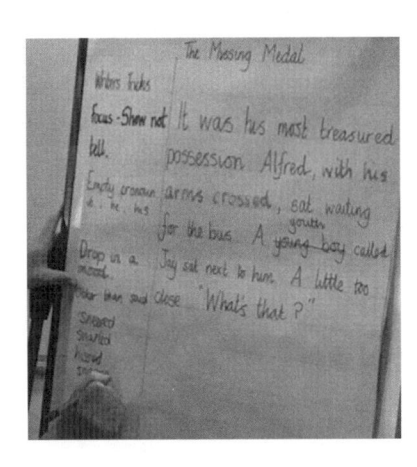

Many teachers have found that the children's learning is accentuated if the margin is used to annotate the writing, showing which features have been used and the technical terms relating to these features. If the notes and the text they relate to can be colour coded, this can be even more powerful. The example here is from St Joseph's, Derby. The margin notes act as a form of toolkit, to help the children understand the ingredients that have been used to make the writing effective.

The quality of the shared writing will determine the progress the children make. Shared writing must be interactive – if it is not, it rivals watching paint dry. One useful approach is to provide the children with mini-white boards on which they are regularly required to jot down ideas, often following opportunities to share ideas with a partner in order to provide thinking time, as illustrated here by a pupil from St Joseph's.

Shared writing is central to the process. Without it, writing is not being taught. The children have to experience the thoughts that go through a writer's head as they try to select just the right word or phrase to express exactly what they are trying to say. This helps the children generate a range of language choices. What changes would make it more effective? The most important thing is to constantly model for the children the importance of reading their work aloud to check first that it flows and, secondly, that it sounds right. This helps the children move from generating to judging. It is worth remembering that there is no such thing as a wow word. The power of a word or a sentence depends on the context it is in. Equally, there never was such thing as a 'Level 5 connective'; but there very much is an effective linking phrase used appropriately in context that can help bring writing to a higher level.

Constant re-reading helps to ensure that the writing flows coherently as well as being a chance to spot mistakes or clumsy writing that jars on the ear. Part of the success of writing is the ability to capture the 'tune' of the text type so that the sentences flow rhythmically in the right register. Pausing to reread helps children 'hear' where editing is needed.

As explained earlier, boxing up is a useful strategy because it encourages children to write in paragraphs. Meanwhile, the toolkits help the children to link their text effectively and write engaging sentences in a manner that is appropriate to the audience and purpose of the text bearing in mind the intended 'reader'. We use our writing style to create the effect.

Occasionally, the teacher will wish to 'demonstrate' during the composition. This means that the teacher explains aloud some new or difficult feature that is being introduced to the children. Often aspects of progress are introduced in this way so that the teacher shows children how to do something, before letting them have a go together until ultimately children attempt something similar independently.

The final text is read through and edited. It helps to make the odd mistake or build in a typical weakness so that a discussion may be opened up that relates to something that the children then look for in their own writing.

Always plan your shared writing. It is worth bearing in mind that shared and guided writing are teaching episodes so they need to be well planned in advance – see **video clip 30** on planning a week's shared, guided and independent writing. It is useful to write out your own version, ensuring that it is pitched at the right level, including the features that you wish to draw to the children's attention. Of course, the children will generate different ideas but the pre-written text gives the teacher both confidence and a useful reminder to focus on any specific teaching points. For example, if a key purpose of the shared writing is to demonstrate how to use adverbs powerfully, you may want to use the gap technique where you write a simple sentence and leave a gap for the appropriate adverb as in: *The strange-looking animal was ...... not a pet*. When you ask the children what word could fill that gap, you are looking for adverbs like *definitely, certainly, decidedly,* *absolutely* etc. However, a child may very well suggest the word *wild* to fill the gap. This is clearly an excellent suggestion so credit it and suggest that they use it when they write but keep searching for appropriate adverbs to accentuate *not* because this was your teaching focus. If every suggestion, however good, is followed willy-nilly, the learning focus will be lost.

Moreover, shared writing is not a question of quickly just doing the introduction. The teacher has to show, through involving the class in the process, how to write the whole text. **Handout 10** focuses on the art of shared writing. It lists all the ingredients that contribute to successful shared writing. It may be useful to look at this list and reflect on which aspects you think you do well and which ones may need sharpening up. Ideally, be brave enough to have yourself filmed while shared writing and reflect on what aspects have worked really well and what aspects might need improving. The earlier you do this in your teaching career the better: the children will benefit from the improved quality of the shared writing and you will be able to concentrate more on your teaching style and less on how old/fat you look!

Moving away from the model – the road to real independence

Shared writing should be developed progressively to illustrate to children how to move further and further away from the model. More confident writers, particularly in years 5 and 6, should be innovating in such a way that, when they write, they use and adapt the underlying structure in different ways while using the related writing toolkit(s) to create the effects they want. Indeed, while their writing is arising from direct teaching through the shared writing, it is in many ways moving towards independent application. Very confident writers might launch straight into their writing and be brought onto the carpet for a review on the second or third day. In this way, the teacher may gradually adapt the pattern of teaching to challenge and support different children. Having said that, where standards are modest, the children will need to hug closer to the model and its underlying structure for longer.

There are many different ways to innovate on a text. It is worth considering which form of innovation is appropriate for the class and children that you teach. At first, most teachers cling too tightly to the model and over-control children's writing. While this may happen with the first couple of innovations when a teacher first uses Talk for Writing, it is important to become more adventurous otherwise the teaching will hold back the writing.

To put it simply, in upper key stage 2 (ages 9–11), children should NOT be using simple substitution or hugging closely to a model unless they are new to the country or have very particular needs. They should be using and adapting the underlying text structure and related toolkit(s) and becoming increasingly creative with their compositions, drawing on their wider reading, ideas and imagination. By the same token, more confident children at key stage 1 (ages 5–7) will be writing text based on the original but increasingly adding and altering so that they have drawn upon the full range of their reading and imagination.

Levels of innovation

Young children can have great fun retelling a text and making it their own by choosing simple substitutions. Reception children love getting involved changing names, places, objects or creatures. By the same token, older children who struggle may benefit from this simple form of substitution that is known as 'hugging closely' – see **video clip 28**. At this stage, the child sticks very closely to the sentence structure of the original. This should be modelled sentence by sentence so that the children are writing on mini whiteboards as the teacher writes and no one is moving on until sentences are completed and punctuation sorted. For example:

Model text	Shared writing – hugging closely	Child's version
Once upon a time, there was a little boy called Charlie **who** lived in a big, big city. **One day, when** he woke up, his mother said to him, "Take this bag to your grandmother."	**Once upon a time**, there was a little girl called Karla **who** lived in a small village. **One day, when** she woke up, her father said to her, "Take this box to your great aunt."	**Once upon a time**, there was a small boy called Kian **who** lived next to the sea. **One day, when** he woke up, his big brother said to him, "Take this rucksack to your uncle."

'Hugging closely' gives confidence but for more confident writers it would be boring and become a trap that limits writing. Once children have grasped simple substitution, they can be shown how to embellish by adding additional detail

> *A long, long time ago, when dragons still roamed the earth, there lived an extremely small girl whose name was Ruby. She lived in a small, small house right under a high, high mountain. **One day, just as she woke up**, her father whispered to her, "Take this secret box to your grandfather's farm."*

As a result, the writer would still hug closely but begin to embellish.

> *A very long time ago, when dinosaurs had only just disappeared, there lived an unusual boy with magic powers. He lived in a tumbledown shack in the shadow of a sugarloaf mountain. **One misty morning, as he lay sleeping, his big brother woke him** by thrusting a small bag into his hand and signalling to him to be silent. "Take the bag to your Great Aunt's house," he whispered, "but don't let anyone see it."*

40 CREATING STORYTELLERS AND WRITERS

Over time, the children will have been shown how to add in and add on to the text to achieve different effects as well as how to change viewpoint, tense and text type – see **video clip 31** supported by **Handout 12** that accompanies the clip. The aim is to achieve confident writers who can manipulate their text engagingly in whatever direction the audience and purpose requires. For example, the teacher could model how to spin the story round so that the story now starts near the end with the main character reflecting ruefully on what he has done:

> *As Charlie placed the chocolate wrapper carefully into his bag, he suddenly realised that there was actually no food left for his grandmother. His mother's parting words rang out in his ears: "Don't you go eating any of that food, now! Remember, it's for granny, not you!"*
>
> *He walked and he walked and he walked more slowly now, desperately rehearsing plausible excuses.*

In the following example, the basic idea still lurks under the writing but this confident writer is now embellishing and experimenting by building description and adding personal responses.

> *Kian checked nervously as he peered out of the front door hoping that no one had seen him hiding a small bag inside the torn lining of his jacket. His brother's alarming instructions rang in his head: "Take this bag to the hermit in the wood. Do not look inside it and on no account let anyone see it."*
>
> *Initially, he had been too scared to peek into the bag himself in his hurry to conceal it. But, as he ventured deeper and deeper into the wood, curiosity began to overcome his caution.*

The temptation for the teacher and the child is to stay with substitution and 'hugging closely' because this gives the illusion of success but true independence and development in writing will not occur unless children move on to adding and altering, drawing on their full range of reading and working at their imaginative fingertips. At Watermoor Primary in Cirencester, they call this 'shaking hands'. In other words, the children decide which parts of a text should they 'hug closely' and where can they 'shake hands' with the text, which means moving away and making it more their own.

If we look at the extended model story 'Thog', it begins in this way: *It had been a long climb up the mountain and, at last, Thog had reached the summit. Thog sat by the cairn at the top of the ridge and stared down the slope towards the distant forest. Somewhere in there was his destination, the stone tower. Word had reached the dwarves that the beekeeper, Olafson, was sick and needed the root of hemp's foot.*

The experienced writer can quickly tell that here we have the beginning of a journey story. The main character, Thog, is already on his way, heading to the stone tower to bring Olafson medicine. Several years ago, this story was used by an experienced teacher with a class of higher attaining writers. Hugging closely would not have been appropriate at all so, in the shared writing, the teacher modelled the notion of using the basic idea of sending a main character on a quest but did not refer directly to the model. Here is the shared writing of the opening:

> *Radiant light struck the mosaic floor of the ruined abbey as Angelo slung his Apollo's bow across his shoulder, in preparation for his long awaited quest. Wrapping his wolf skin cape (cloak) around his numb body, Angelo swung open the arched, oak door. The perishing wind crept and whimpered, almost sweeping him off his unsteady feet.*

You can only just tell that it comes from the same model. In this case, the opening paragraph introduces us to the main character and sets the scene as Angelo prepares to set off on his journey. Where or why, we have yet to discover.

Now let us look at the openings to three stories from this same class. They were all written during this opening lesson. The children are definitely 'shaking hands' with the model, using the basic idea but each one takes their own tack. The first opening is by Samuel and involves a character called Bugdom!

Samuel's version: *Bugdom's Journey*

> *Tightly tying his shoe laces, Bugdom checked that all his necessaries were packed. He had been summoned by the Ladybird kingdom to free their Royal Family who had been captured by the Red Ant colony. He looked out in front of him towards the deserted wildness of the luscious garden. He was ready. Cautiously, Bugdom edged out of the palace and took the first steps of his quest.*
>
> *It had been an hour since he had left and still the whole garden was quiet. Too quiet.*

The repetition of 'too quiet' is most effective and begins to build the tension. This is a good example of a child drawing on a suspense toolkit. In the next example, Chloe has two characters and a horse called Lightning. She introduces the idea of a map and the knotty problem of defeating a plague!

Chloe's version: *Fall of The Plague*

> *The sun was just a finger's breadth over the horizon as Tom, Amy and Lightning left the wizard's tower. Peering down at the magical map (a souvenir from the wizard), they planned their route. Tucking the map in Lightning's bag, Tom and Amy jumped upon his saddle. As the rickety bridge lowered, they made their way through the ill*

> *cheering crowd. "For the King!" they applauded awaiting approval. The harsh wind tugged at Lightning's wavy hair as they set off on their quest to defeat the plague.*
>
> *All that could be heard was the gentle cantering of Lightning's hooves and the spitting of stones, as dust weaved between them.*

The third example, by Henry, is packed with ideas and may need some editing for clarification but he obviously enjoys creating this world where pixies just do not worry enough! Perhaps he has been reading Artemis Fowl?

Henry's version: *The Journey*

> *'Clink'. Martin could still hear the letterbox ringing in his ears. That was the sound that changed his – Martin Valdez, backstreet boy of Brookside's – life, that was the day when everything changed …*
>
> *A sharp shriek raised him from his slumber. Glancing around, Martin discovered where the ear-splitting shriek had come from. It was from Caw the crow, perched upon the tip of the cactus which was one of the only chances of shade in the whole desert. Carefully placing his hand-woven silk sheet into his backpack, Martin produced a flint knife from his jacket – its curved blade the same length from his wrist to his finger tips and its leather binding fitted perfectly for his slender fingers.*
>
> *"Hurry up!" hissed Raven pausing momentarily before darting round the granite stone pillar toward the kitchens. (Her steps so graceful on the uneven flagstones.) The only sound that would give her away was the light padding of her delicate shoes.*
>
> *"I'm coming, just don't get caught!" I moaned to myself.*
>
> *"You worry too much!" laughed Raven who had now appeared by the ancient oak door. Pixies! They don't worry enough.*

In this class, constant deep reading, high quality shared writing and a strong sense of commitment to writing has developed young writers mastering their craft. The shared writing is showing the children how to take an underlying plot idea and draw on the writing toolkits to create their own stories. This work is at the 'innovation' stage and the teacher is still using shared writing to involve the children in high-level composition. Once these stories have been completed, the children will then have the chance to write totally independently. They will have the advantage of the original model, the shared writing acting as a model as well as the sharing of their classmates' stories. This happens because, at the end of the innovation stage, the children sit in 'story circles' and each child reads aloud a chosen part of their story.

The more that the children move away from the model and begin to just use the basic plot idea and related writing toolkit(s), the more they become independent as writers. In some sessions, they will be working on new aspects of writing but in many they will be expected to move away from the comfort of a model. Otherwise, the model is no longer a scaffold but becomes a constraint.

Hugging closely ➡ Independent application ➡ Some original additions

It is important to move children through different forms of innovation so that they are increasingly challenged but also gain confidence in manipulating what they know so that they can create something new. Innovation is about practising transferable language patterns that, in the end, children will be able to draw upon in order to create. Make sure that you make the following patterns explicit:

- **Big text patterns**, *e.g. journey stories/portal stories (see **Handouts 5a & b**)*
- **Toolkits**, *e.g. how to make writing tense, etc. (see **Appendix 2**)*
- **Basic written style**, *e.g. word choice, sentence variation, etc.*

By year 6, they should have mastered the various ingredients of the different text types so that they would be able to transfer text that has been presented say in narrative style and convert it into news recount or information. Over time, they should be able to write much more sophisticated text and to mix and match text features as appropriate because, in real life, pure text type is rare; most texts are an amalgam.

Children plan and write their own version

Shared writing is then followed immediately by the children attempting their own composition – perhaps working on the writing over several days, section by section. The more the children have been taught to love language and savour new words, the more they will enjoy their writing. The picture here shows a boy at Selby Community Primary totally absorbed in his writing. In **video clip 32**, you can hear him and his writing partner talking about their love of words and writing; the boy pictured here had only been in this country for two years at the time of this interview. Most importantly, the Talk for Writing process engages the children:

> *It makes me feel like I'm going to be a writer. I like making a new version of it (the text). It helps me with my writing and my imagination.* – Sarrinah, Harbour Centre, Staines

> *Yes, I like writing more because I like the flow of writing. It feels good in a way. I'm concentrating and listening more and that has helped my writing.*
> – Hope, pupil from Lewisham Talk for Writing across the curriculum project

Peer assessment

Once they have completed a paragraph, ask the children to share their work with a partner and read it through together discussing what works and what might need improving alongside making certain there are no basic errors like missing full stops or capital letters. The picture shows two children at Penn Wood Primary, Slough, totally engaged in reflecting on their work. Many teachers have found the two-colour approach useful here – say pink for perfect and green for growth. These colours can be used by the children and their teacher alike when reflecting on work. The colours chosen don't matter as long as there is consistency across the school. Whatever assessment system you choose, be sure to keep it simple and focused on the children improving their work – see **Handout 4**.

The teacher can then assess the work and adapt the following day's shared writing in the light of what the children need. Once the work has been completed, you might want to ask the children to read their work through, checking it carefully, and write their own comment about how well they think they have completed the task. This is a good way of ensuring the children become increasingly responsible for the quality of their own work and correcting their own errors; it also gets the dialogue going about what needs to be done to improve their work.

Next steps based on assessment

When assessing the work, teachers need to consider two key aspects:

- How well did the children tackle the writing as writers?
- How effective was the writing?

The answers to these questions will inform the next piece of teaching which should be focused on what the children need in order to improve. Do they need to work on the actual business of being a writer – gathering and sorting ideas, concentrating whilst writing, referring to the plan as well as their journals, or editing. Additionally, what is there in the actual writing that has worked well and what needs to be attended to next in order to improve?

The 'marking'/'assessment for learning' should clearly let the child know what has worked well but also point them towards what needs to be done next – see **video clip 33**. This allows the teacher to increasingly draw the children into working together to develop their repertoire as writers. The assessment also helps to focus the teacher on what needs to be emphasised in the independent application stage. Which language features require further embedding before the children can attempt to apply what they have learnt independently?

The teacher can then decide which features to revisit and strengthen later and which feature will be focused on immediately the work is handed back to the children. If this feature has been identified say by a simple green line down the relevant section in the margin, then the teacher can begin the lesson with an activity related to this feature. When the books are given back, the children can immediately improve this aspect of their work. If work that has been marked is handed back and the children aren't immediately required to improve it, then all the time spent marking has been wasted.

To provide feedback, 'visualisers', iPads, or any other electronic method of getting the children's work on screen, are very powerful. This means that the teacher and the children can use the children's writing to consider what has worked well and to discuss what needs to be improved. **Handout 11** is full of phrases supporting self- assessment and may be useful here. The teacher models the language to help the children reflect on what works and what needs to be improved so that the children learn to use the same phrases and reflect on their work and the work of others. After such support, a pupil's work could be projected on screen and the author explain the choices that they have made followed by the class being involved in suggesting possible improvements. The more practice the children get at reflecting on the quality of work and how to improve it, the more they will develop their own editing skills – see **video clip 34**.

The teacher can model how to be a successful 'response partner' with the whole class and display useful phrases to enable the children to reflect on their partner's work and their own. The picture here shows how Front Lawn Academy, Havant, provides pupils with the sort of sentence patterns they will need when commenting on each other's work. Mini whiteboards are also a useful resource for getting children to reflect on possible improvements and feedback their ideas.

Such activities enable children to develop their inner judge that will help them decide how to edit their own work.

The basic routine for being a response partner is as follows:

- The author reads their work to their partner, perhaps explaining what they were trying to do
- The partner discusses with the author what 'works well'
- One or two places might be identified where improvements could be made
- Final decisions are always left to the author
- Time is then provided to allow the author to make the changes they have selected.

If the children's work lacks coherent links, the best activity to support their development with this key feature is sentence combination. This involves providing the children with a series of simple sentences in logical but unconnected order about whatever topic is being focused. For example:

The man sat down. He was curious. He had seen the metal box. He wondered what was inside. He was calm.

The task is to combine them into coherent well-linked sentences. *See Jumpstart! Grammar* for more examples of this important technique. The *Bill and Betty* tactic is another good idea to use at this point. At break time the teacher (in role as Bill or Betty) puts work up on the flipchart that mirrors the errors typically made by the children. The children's job, once break is over, is to suggest how the work can be improved. One teacher famously reported hearing one boy saying, in all seriousness, that Bill's writing seemed to be improving.

Mini lessons can also be useful at this juncture.   For example, if three key issues have emerged when the teacher is marking the books, the teacher may decide to offer 3 different surgeries: one run by them; one by the TA and one by a pupil who has excelled at the feature being focused on. There are several possible formats but the two below are the most obvious:

- *'I want these children to come to join me for a mini lesson on ...'*
- *'This morning there will be 3 mini lessons – but you can only come to one – choose the one that you feel you most need to attend.'*

These are usually short-burst and very focused; the children then adapt their writing immediately.

Chapter 4: Independent application and real independence

> 3. Independent application
>
> - Next steps based on assessment
> - Pupils write independently
>
> *Hot task*

In this final stage of the process, the children move towards becoming more independent, as illustrated by **video clip 35**.

Initially, this was called **Invention**. However, Talk for Writing is a constantly developing process as ideas are refined by practice. Action research and reflection has changed how the process is described because, at this final stage, the children are not inventing but are showing their ability to independently use the features focused on in the unit. Time needs to be set aside in between taught units to allow the children the chance to choose how and what they write and develop their writing skills in any way they want. This is invention and leads to real independence as a writer as explained at the end of this chapter.

For the independent application stage, let us imagine that the children have been working on Little Charlie. They have already innovated on the text and written their own version. Now, following the assessment of their innovations and the immediate feedback, the teacher has planned a range of activities to strengthen areas where the children were having difficulties. The class has brainstormed a range of adventurous ways for innovating on the story and embellishing it to make it more engaging and may have practised orally rehearsing their ideas. Now the children have the chance to plan and write their version on their own showing what they have learnt about making such a story engaging.

The teacher may still decide to use shared writing to teach features that need strengthening but has the advantage of having read the children's stories at the innovation stage and observed them in the course of writing. This means that the shared writing now can focus on aspects of the process that need reinforcing as well as aspects of the actual writing that need revisiting and strengthening. The assessment drives the shared writing and allows the teacher to consider what groupings are needed for any additional guided writing or whether more confident groups can immediately move into independent application.

Another aspect of this stage that can be very productive is to throw into the melting pot several more models so that the children can consider how different writers tackle writing similar text type. This might allow children to add more to the list of ingredients or techniques thereby beginning to broaden their repertoire.

The children can then use their boxing-up skills to start planning their independent work around the same writing focus. They can use their text-mapping skills to populate their boxed-up planner with ideas. They can then talk their text with their partner and adapt their ideas in the light of this if they choose. Then, when they begin to write, they will know what they are trying to say and how they want to say it.

Once again, when they have finished their independent writing, they could read it aloud and discuss it with a partner, improve it as they think best, give it a final check through and write a comment on how well they think they have written the piece.

This stage of independent application might look somewhat different with different classes. Confident writers may need additional high-quality shared writing as a focus. This might be supported by 'reading as writers' a variety of high-level texts which can then be drawn upon and imitated. Less confident classes may have to revisit the whole process of gathering their information, drawing and telling before moving into boxing up, and rehearsing ideas followed by shared, guided and then independent writing. Some children may be best advised to 'hug closely' to the original model. The amount of scaffolding required is in direct relation to what the children need in order to get success. The important thing is to work towards weaning them off the scaffolding.

Was the writing effective?

In many schools, teachers are, sadly, driven to teach whatever is the latest version of levels rather than teaching writing. The language of the professional SATs or grammar test marker has crept into the classroom and, rather than children writing in order to communicate powerfully, they write to achieve a level or proficiency in the use of some disembodied grammar feature like the fronted adverbial. In these circumstances, teaching writing is reduced to the level of a checklist of features that have to be included – whether they enhanced or detracted from the effectiveness of the writing seems to have become irrelevant.

Whenever the children write, they must be encouraged to read their work through and try to ensure that it is engaging the reader so that it fulfils its purpose: the suspense really does make the reader anxious; the character description really does make the reader picture the person described etc.

The creative generation of sentences in writing should be balanced constantly by rereading to listen to whether it 'sounds right' – whether powerful communication is developing. Often, you can hear whether writing works just by reading it aloud. Sometimes it will be hard to explain why something works or does not – and you have to resort to saying, 'Well, it just doesn't sound quite right'. One boy referred to this as 'testing out our writing'. This means that an important aspect of the writing process will be reading writing aloud to a partner or in a circle. Usually, teachers do this after the children have finished writing but it can be very helpful during the writing – perhaps after each paragraph. In the end, the key questions have to be:

- Does the writing fulfil its brief at the level of composition and effect?
- Does it tell the reader what happened in an interesting, amusing and engaging way that will make them want to read on?

Ultimately, the final copy may be put into a booklet, onto the school's website, displayed or turned into some form of presentation. This encourages an attention to detail and focuses the mind on the need to present writing as accurately and powerfully as possible, taking good account of the need to engage an audience. Look at this year 6 classroom display from Warren Road Primary of the suspense element of a warning story based on Little Red Riding Hood. The quality of the images supporting the text and the quality of the layout of the display is immediately engaging. But when you move closer,

does the text disappoint or would it help inspire the children to emulate such techniques themselves? When you read the text below, the child's ability to make the story their own by engaging the reader through well-crafted, well-punctuated, varied sentence structures and vocabulary choices shines through. As the mother's warning reverberates in the scared child's mind, the reader is hooked and wants to read on.

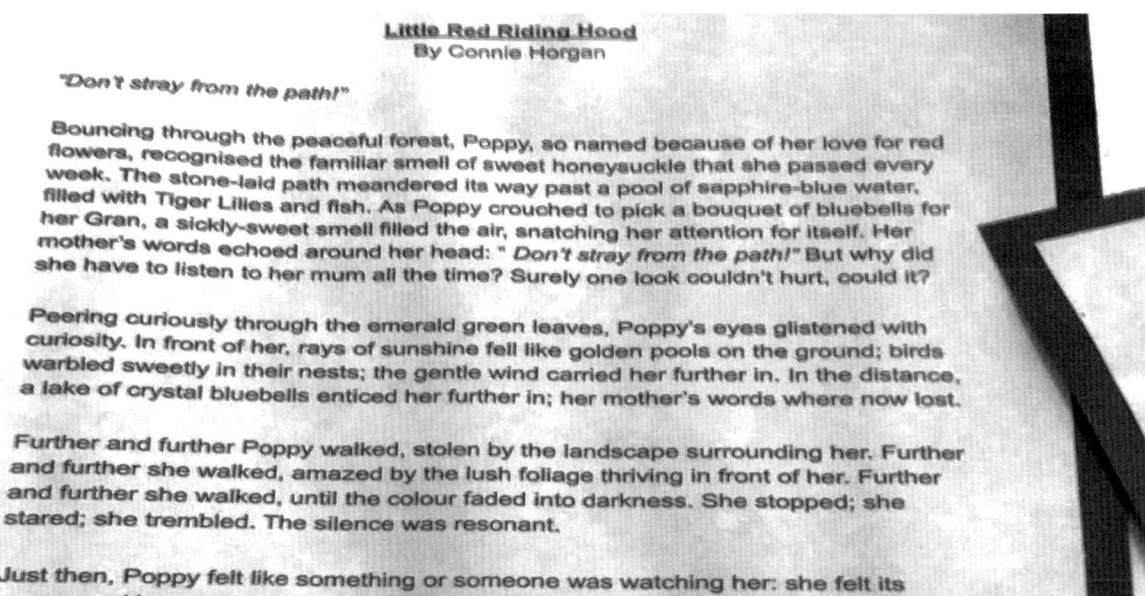

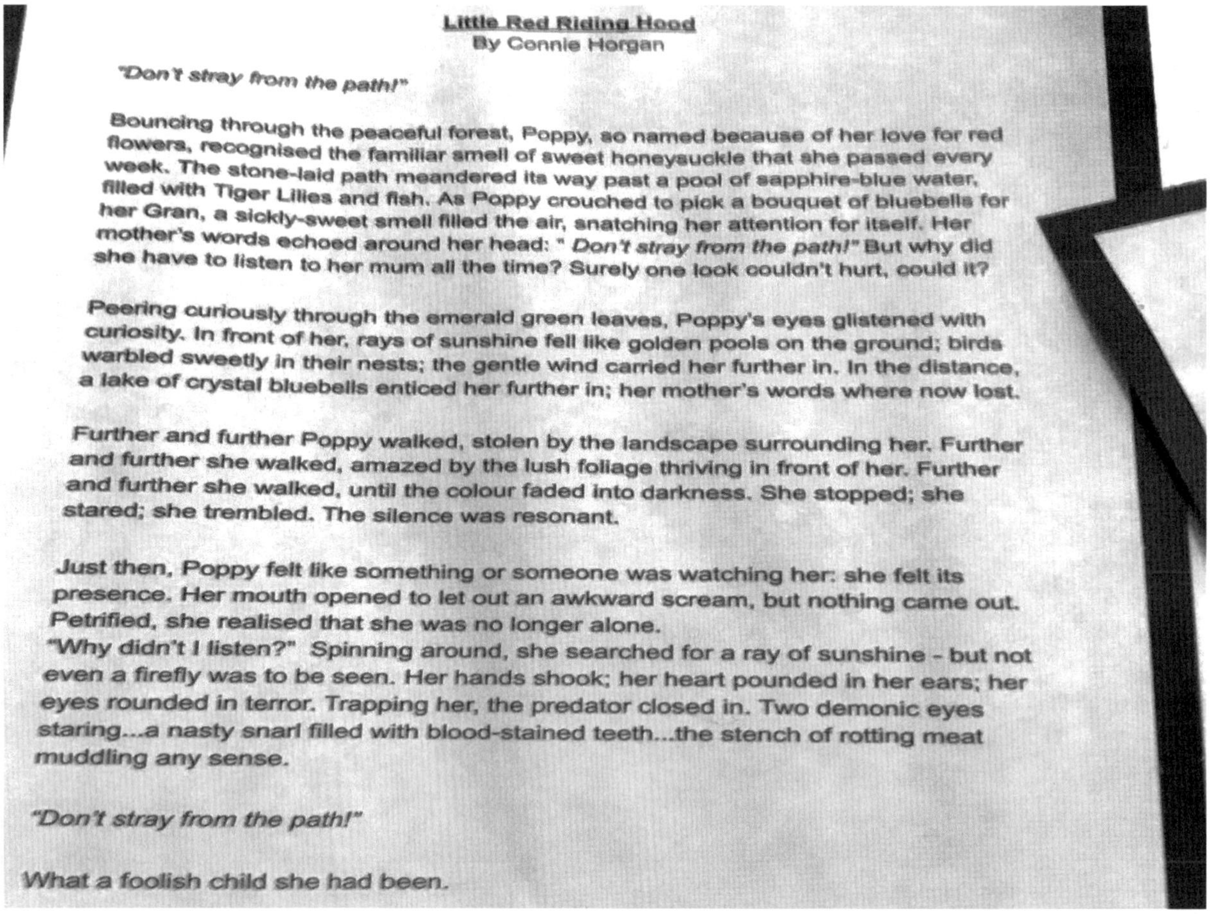

50 CREATING STORYTELLERS AND WRITERS

Little Red Riding Hood
By Connie Horgan

"Don't stray from the path!"

Bouncing through the peaceful forest, Poppy, so named because of her love for red flowers, recognised the familiar smell of sweet honeysuckle that she passed every week. The stone-laid path meandered its way past a pool of sapphire-blue water, filled with Tiger Lilies and fish. As Poppy crouched to pick a bouquet of bluebells for her Gran, a sickly-sweet smell filled the air, snatching her attention for itself. Her mother's words echoed around her head: " *Don't stray from the path!*" But why did she have to listen to her mum all the time? Surely one look couldn't hurt, could it?

Peering curiously through the emerald green leaves, Poppy's eyes glistened with curiosity. In front of her, rays of sunshine fell like golden pools on the ground; birds warbled sweetly in their nests; the gentle wind carried her further in. In the distance, a lake of crystal bluebells enticed her further in; her mother's words where now lost.

Further and further Poppy walked, stolen by the landscape surrounding her. Further and further she walked, amazed by the lush foliage thriving in front of her. Further and further she walked, until the colour faded into darkness. She stopped; she stared; she trembled. The silence was resonant.

Just then, Poppy felt like something or someone was watching her: she felt its presence. Her mouth opened to let out an awkward scream, but nothing came out. Petrified, she realised that she was no longer alone.
"Why didn't I listen?" Spinning around, she searched for a ray of sunshine – but not even a firefly was to be seen. Her hands shook; her heart pounded in her ears; her eyes rounded in terror. Trapping her, the predator closed in. Two demonic eyes staring...a nasty snarl filled with blood-stained teeth...the stench of rotting meat muddling any sense.

"Don't stray from the path!"

What a foolish child she had been.

The end of unit assessment – assessing progress

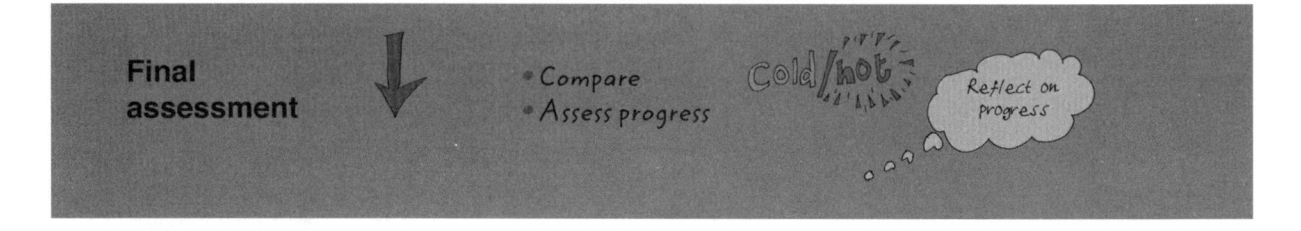

Final assessment → • Compare • Assess progress   Cold/hot   Reflect on progress

This independent writing can act as the **hot task** – showing what the children now know. Once it has been assessed by the teacher, the teacher can look back at each child's **cold task** to assess what progress has been made, as explained on pages 7-9. The teacher can then decide what general language features will need to be particularly focused on in the next unit in English as well as which features will need to be further developed across the curriculum so that the children have the opportunity to broaden and deepen the range of their writing. When the work is handed back, apart from focusing on whatever feature the teacher has selected for the children to improve, the children can then look at their cold task and at the hot task and reflect on the progress they have made. This process, when properly developed, is highly motivating.

Here is a year 4 pupil's cold task from Hallsville Primary, Newham, having being given a picture of two characters in a magical setting and asked to write a conversation between them. As you can see, left to their own devices, this pupil

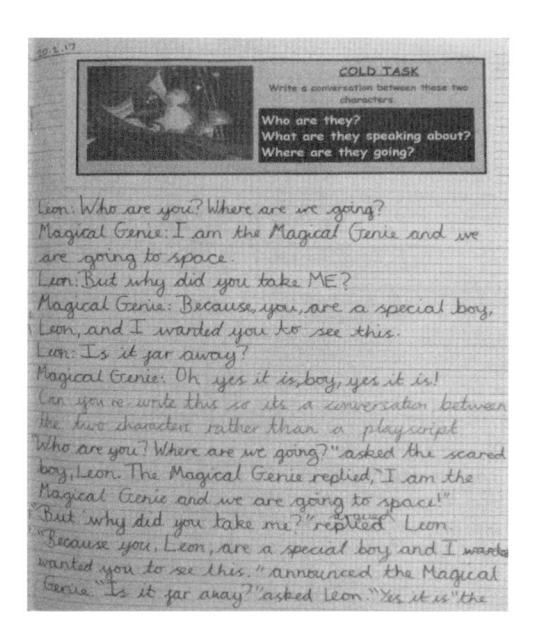

INDEPENDENT APPLICATION AND REAL INDEPENDENCE 51

has written this in play format with no stage directions. The reader is somewhat grateful that it is short. However, the punctuation is good and certainly the writer is showing promise. The teacher, underneath the initial attempt, has requested a conversation rather than a playscript. The result is a conversation but with too much dialogue with little or no intervening description to keep the reader engaged. The writer knew to start a new line for each speaker in a play but does not know to start a new paragraph for each speaker in a story. Now look at the same pupil's hot task:

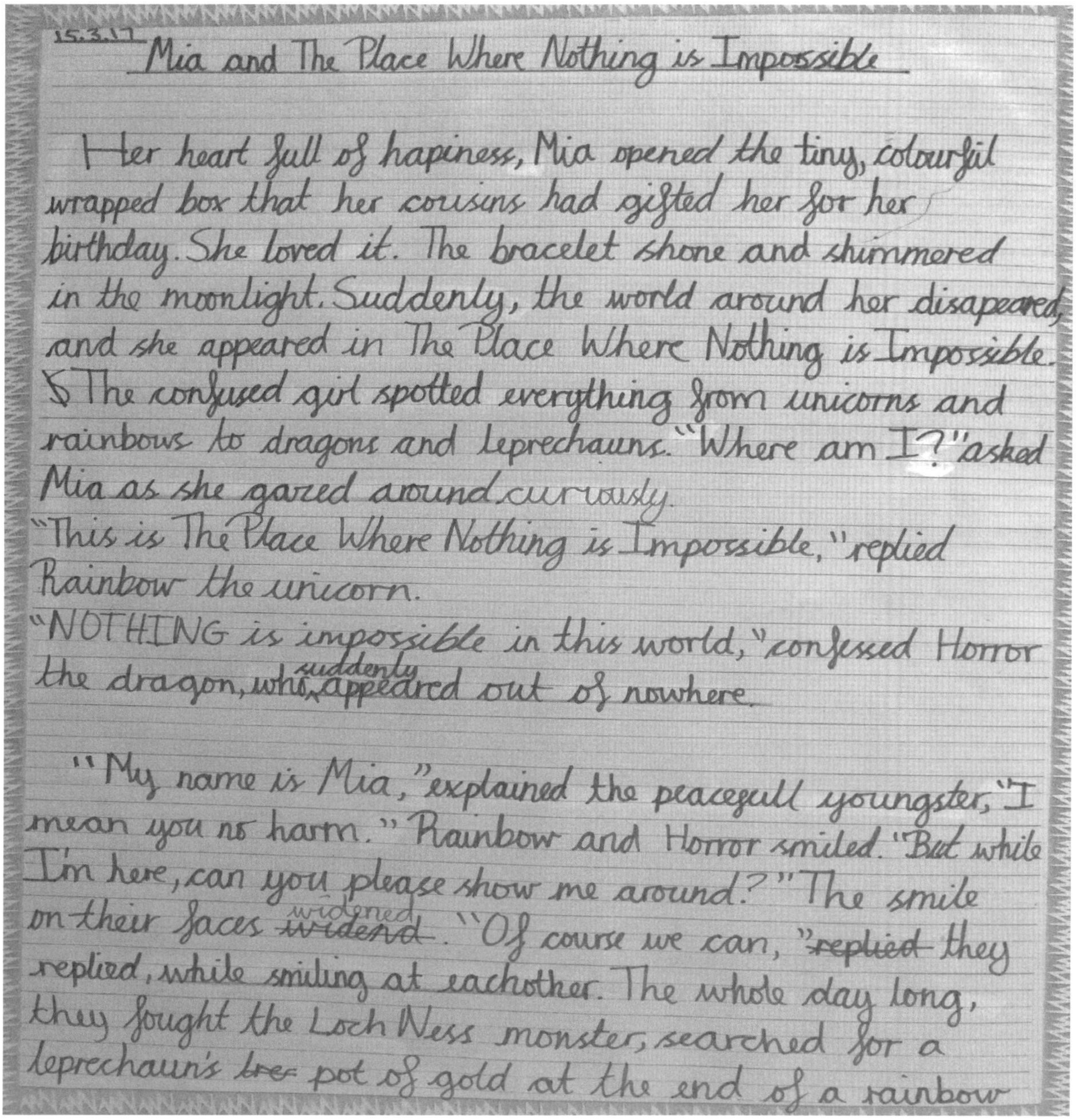

Mia and The Place Where Nothing is Impossible

Her heart full of hapiness, Mia opened the tiny, colourful wrapped box that her cousins had gifted her for her birthday. She loved it. The bracelet shone and shimmered in the moonlight. Suddenly, the world around her disapeared, and she appeared in The Place Where Nothing is Impossible. The confused girl spotted everything from unicorns and rainbows to dragons and leprechauns. "Where am I?" asked Mia as she gazed around curiously.

"This is The Place Where Nothing is Impossible," replied Rainbow the unicorn.

"NOTHING is impossible in this world," confessed Horror the dragon, who suddenly appeared out of nowhere.

"My name is Mia," explained the peacefull youngster, "I mean you no harm." Rainbow and Horror smiled. "But while I'm here, can you please show me around?" The smile on their faces widened. "Of course we can," replied they replied, while smiling at eachother. The whole day long, they fought the Loch Ness monster, searched for a leprechaun's pot of gold at the end of a rainbow

You can clearly see the progress made in writing skills. The sentence structures, particularly the openings, are varied and engaging, the description is vivid and effective and the dialogue is well integrated into the story and reveals character without dominating the story so that the reader wants to read on. The understanding of beginning a new paragraph for each speaker began well but then faded out – clearly something that needs further practice. The reader can picture the skills that have been introduced and embedded in this unit to provide the pupil with the skills they are now illustrating.

One good way of testing whether the children really have internalised the writing features concentrated on within a unit is to wait a month or so and then set a similar writing task and see if they can still do it independently.

Achieving real independence through creativity and invention

Children never become independent readers until they choose what to read, developing their own taste for different authors and styles; in the same way, children are not writers until they make their own choices about what to write.

If children are to become effective creative writers who enjoy writing, they will need the motivation that comes from being able to choose their own topic and writing about it as they choose. At the end of units, it is a good idea to plan in free writing opportunities when the children know in advance that they will have the freedom to write in any way they select about what interests them drawing on everything that they have been taught – see **video clip 36** and **Handouts 2a & b**. One school where they have adopted such an approach, and where the children know that in the coming week they will have free choice, reports that the children come running into school on Monday morning full of enthusiasm to do the writing that they have chosen to plan across the weekend.

The Talk for Writing process (summed up by **video clip 37**) enables pupils to hone their skills in a wide range of text. To nurture creativity and invention in writing, time needs to be found for pupils to develop these skills freely so that they can create the type of text they choose about a topic of their choice. In this way, genuine inventiveness and originality will be encouraged.

Here are a few examples of KS2 units that provide time for children to write entirely independently drawing on the taught units. Start from a great stimulus and then list the possibilities with the class. They can then choose from this list or devise for themselves what to write and how to write it. Provide a number of days for them to plan, draft, edit and publish their own writing.

Example 1: 'Stranded' – the children have been shipwrecked on a desert island. The children could:
- draw maps of the island; write diary entries and stories about the storm, logging the first few days of survival and even the rescue
- find images of desert islands and write an advert for an island holiday
- invent their own island – draw the map and write a leaflet about its flora and fauna
- write a monologue revealing the stranded sailor's wishes and dreams, hopes and fears
- write the sea captain's log depicting the rescue
- Imagine that the ship's cat is also rescued; write a recount in the role of the cat!
- write an alphabet of things found on the island, etc.

Example 2: 'The Lighthouse' – use the short film 'The Lighthouse' from the Literacy Shed. The children could:
- write the story of what happened from the viewpoint of the lighthouse keeper/ the ship's captain/ a cabin boy or one of the villagers
- the event could be written up as a newspaper article or the keeper's log
- write a poem about 'the storm'
- write explanations of other ideas for saving the ship
- write a list with 'ten ways to stop a lighthouse keeper from being bored'
- find out about lighthouses and write a fact file
- design the perfect lighthouse
- write the story that explains why the keeper is alone in the lighthouse, etc.

Example 3: 'Voices in the Park' – respond to this great picture book (or any other decent picture book or novel). The children could:
- write diary entries in role as different characters
- write a short play based on the characters chatting at a bus stop
- write letters between the two children
- write about what happened from a park keeper's viewpoint
- write a letter from the father persuading the mother to let the children play together – and then write the reply
- create the newspaper that the man is reading
- write a letter that the mother has in her handbag
- write about what you think will happen to the four main characters
- write about the adults from the dog's view!
- write a 'transformation list poem' in which park objects turn into other things, *e.g. In the park, the roundabout becomes / a Catherine wheel sending out golden sparks. In the park, a tree becomes / a flame shimmering in the autumn air.*

Example 3: The Adventures of Harris Burdick – this wonderful book consists of a sequence of unrelated and rather disturbing images. Children choose one to use as a basis for writing. For example:
- If the chosen image is the front cover, what would the story title be? Write the story
- Put 2 images together and link them
- Write the story about Harris Burdick, explaining why he never returned!
- Take an image and write just the paragraph that goes with it. Then write the paragraph before and what happened next so that you have a mini story of 3 paragraphs.

Resources

- *Talk for Writing Across the Curriculum* by Pie Corbett and Julia Strong. Published by The Open University Press. The essential guide to extending the approach into non-fiction text and right across the curriculum, including 2 DVDs to support school training plus worked examples of how to apply the approach to the key non-fiction text types.
- *Talk for Writing in the Early Years* by Pie Corbett and Julia Strong. Published by The Open University Press. The essential guide to introducing the approach from nursery to KS1, including 2 DVDs to support school training plus an explanation of how to make storytelling interactive and how to involve the families.
- *Jumpstart! Grammar* by Pie Corbett and Julia Strong. Published by Routledge (a David Fulton Book). Essential reading and reference book for any teacher trying to get their head round how to engage children with grammar. Full of entertaining activities to be integrated into units of work.
- *Writing Models Year 3/ Year 4/ Year 5/ Year 6* by Pie Corbett. Published by Routledge (a David Fulton Book). Each book is full of useful models that can be adapted to suit your class.
- *Jumpstart! Literacy* by Pie Corbett. Published by Routledge (a David Fulton Book). A long-standing bestseller full of engaging activities to help children warm up and embed the key language focuses of units of work.
- *Jumpstart!* Poetry by Pie Corbett. Published by Routledge (a David Fulton Book). Packed full of engaging games, ideas & models.
- *Jumpstart!* Storymaking by Pie Corbett. Published by Routledge (a David Fulton Book). Packed full of great games, ideas & models.
- *Tell Me* by Aidan Chambers. Published by Thimble Press. An invaluable guide to how to engage children in discussing text.

Appendix 1: How to use the DVDs to support staff training

The DVD footage includes clips of Pie Corbett illustrating the approach at three different Talk for Writing conferences on fiction as well as film of Talk for Writing in action in classrooms around the country. In the conference clips, the text on screen is often hard to read, so the slides have been superimposed on the film. There are various different ways in which the footage might be used. You might want to stage your personal viewing over a number of days, watching snippets alongside reading the accompanying book, till in the end you have seen the whole thing and, in this way, support your personal development in teaching in Talk for Writing style.

However, we envisage that the main use for the DVD would be in staff meetings and Inset days to show how the Talk for Writing approach can help pupils become confident story writers. It will be useful for Teaching Assistants as well as teachers to attend this training because the more all the adults in the classroom understand and support the approach, the more progress the children will make.

It helps considerably if, during training, you can use real examples of writing by children in your school – and it is most powerful if you have film clips of the children using the approach.

There are a variety of clips so that you can tailor the approach to suit the needs of your school. Some of the clips focus on early years and Key Stage 1 pupils, while other clips deal with more sophisticated approaches for older groups illustrating how to achieve quality independent writing that has moved a long way from any original model. Several clips and **Handouts 8, 9 & 10** on shared writing have been included to support extended training on this very important aspect.

Depending on the training you want to focus on, it will be useful for the teachers and teaching assistants to have copies of the handouts that support that section. The relevant handouts are referenced throughout. **Handout 4** on formative assessment is key. Since this underpins the approach, it would be useful to distribute this in advance of any training and ask everyone attending to have read it prior to the training.

DVD 1	
Chapter 1: Introduction	
1: Introducing the underlying principles of Talk for Writing (7 minutes)	*The Talk for Writing process* www.talk4writing.com This film clip combines Pie's introduction to two conferences on fiction. It is probably best used as part of training to introduce the Talk for Writing approach in a school. At **0:53,** pause the clip and ask the teachers and TAs to note down the main points that Pie is making. Then pause at **4:32** and flip chart these up to support a discussion of why they are important. You will probably have made points like these: • Place teaching emphasis on composition and effect rather than on disembodied grammar features • TfW is a whole school system • The text types are taught as units • TfW is based on a logical sequence moving from model to shared writing to children doing similar writing on own • Each lesson builds on the previous lesson based on formative assessment through assessing what the children have done and need to do next • Teaching is explicit so the learning objective is clear • Have high expectations – aim for success for all At **4:33**, Pie introduces the "three eyes": Imitation, Innovation and Invention/Independent application. Explain to your audience that the earlier term Invention has now been replaced by Independent application as stated on page 44. Ask the teachers to note down why the imitation stage is so important and discuss this at the end of the clip. It may be useful to provide your audience with **Handout 1** for this and the next clip as it shows the Talk for Writing process.
2: Talk for Writing overview (7 minutes)	**Clip 2** begins by focusing on the three eyes. You may find it useful to get the teachers to listen to how Pie explains the three "eyes" again to reinforce their understanding of the centrality of the imitation stage to the success of the process.

58 CREATING STORYTELLERS AND WRITERS

		At **9:54**, pause and ask your audience to listen carefully to this next section and be prepared to discuss whether Pie's suggestion of a story bank of 10 stories a year is a useful idea and how it could be implemented. See Pie's Reading Spine published by Scholastic for a useful list of texts to include: https://shop.scholastic.co.uk/piecorbett.
Baseline assessment		
	3: Initial assessment (9 minutes)	This clip provides an explanation of how the initial assessment should guide the planning for the unit. Ask the teachers and TAs, while watching the clip, to think about why it would be a good idea to use this cold-task approach to establish the initial assessment. You may want to follow the clip with a discussion about why and how this could be implemented. It would be a good idea to have provided everyone with a copy of **Handout 4** to read before the training to support this section. It might be useful to pause the clip at **19:02** and provide everyone with a copy of a cold task, like the Year 1 example below from this book (see page 7) where the child had been asked to write a little story about a character they liked. Once there lived a orange and white clown fish. Called phoebe. She lived with her family. In some pink sparkling corell reef. But one day her little sisster got lost in the shipreck. Where a shark lived. She hast save her. But how. Everyone could then have a go at deciding what language targets should be exemplified by the model text and reinforced throughout the related unit of work. This may provide a useful way in to establishing the routine that Pie is suggesting. Pie then reiterates the importance of having units bookended by cold and hot tasks in which anyone can see the progress and shows a helpful example of what this can look like, alongside emphasising the importance of getting the children involved in reflecting on their learning. You may want to use this part of the clip to reinforce the significance of the approach and get teachers to reflect on the importance of having a system that helps the child, the teacher, the parents, senior management and the inspectorate alike to see progress simply by looking in the books.

(margin notes: cold task, Handout, cold task, Hot task)

APPENDIX 1 59

	In addition, you may want to discuss how you are going to set up a routine where everyone collaborates to achieve effective assessment of cold tasks and the related target setting. At **21:10**, just before Pie invites his audience to discuss the idea of bookending units with cold and hot tasks, he suggests that by KS2 children should be writing down their reflections on what they have achieved in a unit and what they now need to focus on. Again, this would be a useful focus for a discussion. If the teachers can see why it is useful, they are much more likely to introduce the idea effectively.
4: Initial assessment for early years (5 minutes)	This clip has been included to show how the cold-to-hot assessment process can be adapted to suit early years children. While watching this section, ask the audience to note down what the system suggested is and then discuss why this might be useful. The two key questions at the beginning of Reception are: • Can you tell me a story you know? • Can you make up a new story and tell it to me? If you want further information on how to introduce the approach in early years, the book to use is *Talk for Writing in the Early Years*. You may also want to pause at **23:43** and ask your audience to note down why it is a good idea to scribe the stories that the children tell and then, at the end of the clip, discuss why this is important. Flipchart the key points and discuss whether in your school scribing children's stories is part of the early years' routine.
Planning	
5: Planning a unit (8 minutes)	This clip provides a very useful overview of the planning process. It would be helpful to provide your audience with copies of **Handouts 2a & 2b** to support their understanding of the planning process Pie is explaining. (Note Pie is referring to handouts 5a & b for his audience – but these are 2a and 2b in this book. He also apologises for the handouts not having short-burst writing on them because of lack of space but your handouts do include this.) You may also want to provide your audience with a copy of the Talk for Writing teaching guide for progression in writing year by year.

cold task

Hot task

Handout

This document can be downloaded from www.talk4writing.co.uk/portfolio-items/year-on-year-progress/ and amended to suit your school.

Note: If Pie were presenting these Overview-of-planning grids today, he would also want to illustrate how free writing units should be slotted in between the taught units – see **pages 52-54** and **video clip 36**. **Handouts 2a & 2b** have therefore been amended to include this feature but Pie does not mention it in clip 5. You may wish to point this feature out but perhaps not discuss it until you show **clip 36**.

The end of this clip is probably the best place to discuss the planning approach that Pie is advocating: i.e. plan language focuses that, over time, cover the key story patterns and related writing techniques (**Handouts 5a & 5b**) as well as the features of the six non-fiction text types as illustrated by the toolkits in **Appendix 2**.

However, you may want to pause at the sections indicated below to discuss these two related points.

At **27:51**, ask the audience to note down why it is important to focus on the language content of English units and not the topic. When you reach **29:27**, pause to discuss this.

At **31:54**, Pie explains that once this planning process has been established, teachers are then liberated to focus on formative assessment to improve the teaching and learning. Pause at the end of the clip to discuss this.

Chapter 2: Imitation stage

6: The hook

(1 minute)

This section provides a useful overview of the importance of having a good hook to motivate the children to engage with a unit and give it an edge of audience and purpose. After viewing the clip, you may want to ask your audience to discuss why the hook is important and what hooks they have used that proved very successful.

	7: Warming up and embedding grammar and spelling (12 minutes)	Embedding grammar within teaching sequences in an engaging way is proving problematic in some schools. It may be worth spending some time on this clip. When watching the opening of the clip, you may want to ask the audience to consider why teaching the grammar and spelling contextually is important and how this can be done by building the features into your model text and related warming up and embedding activities, as well as into the marking. Pause at **40:35** to discuss this. Then show the games that Pie illustrates so people gain confidence in how to use such activities and can see how they could be integrated contextually into units of work. It would be useful to have copies of *Jumpstart! Literacy* and *Jumpstart! Grammar* to support this section. At the end of the clip, it may be useful to give everyone a simple model text that is used in your school and ask them to identify the key grammar features that this model could be used to help teach and then to work on the warming-up games that could accompany it, with the help of this clip and the following clip.	
	8: Warming up the tune of the text (3 minutes)	This is an entertaining clip illustrating a range of activities to help warm up the sentence patterns that help create the tune of a text. You might want to pause the clip at the end of each little game and get the audience to have a quick go at playing the same game themselves. This will give them confidence in integrating such activities into their teaching repertoire. It would be useful to have copies of *Jumpstart! Storymaking* available so that teachers have easy access to a wide range of these activities.	
	9: Teachers warming up the words at Warren Road Primary, Orpington (3 minutes)	This clip of Year 1 teachers from Warren Road Primary, Orpington, will be an effective way of supporting teachers and TAs in how they can warm up the words of a unit and how they can work in partnership so that the vocabulary the children select is written up on the flipchart. You may want to pause at the image of the flipchart at **52:17** and ask the audience why they think these words are on the flipchart. Ask the audience to note down the techniques that the teacher is using to involve the children in expanding the vocabulary and flip chart up their suggestions.	

		You may end up with a list like this:
		- Teacher refers to flipchart toolkit of words they are creating with similar meanings
- Teacher acts out what word means
- Teacher asks children for what it might mean
- Teacher asks the children for the words they liked from what they just heard
- Children come up and present their version of what a crayon quitting would say
- The audience is asked to respond to the vocabulary used by the children presenting their work
- The teacher feeds back the key points the children are making about the other children's choice of words and why it is effective
- The teacher guides the class to remember to include the rhetorical question technique when presenting an argument
	10: Pupil from Warren Road Primary demonstrating the difference it makes (2 minutes)	This clip makes a good follow-on activity to **Clip 9**. Here, a year 1 child is reading her work in the headteacher's office. Before the audience watches this clip, ask them to listen out for the features they would comment on. When the clip has finished, ask them to discuss in small groups and then feed back their main points. You may end up with a list like this:
- Child's engagement with what she has written and the emotions of the piece
- Use of rhetorical question to engage listener/reader
- Wide range of different ways to express how fed up the crayon is
- Pupil has worked with a group of other children
- Pupil has magpied the terms *fly off the handle, exhausted* and *deflated* from others in this group
- Pupil's ability to explain clearly and illustrate what deflated means

Then ask them to think about how the teaching method they have seen has helped produce this result. |

11: **Imitating the model text** (11 minutes)	This is a key clip because Pie is explaining the importance of preparing thoroughly before leading a class in imitating text. You might want to ask the audience to jot down the main points of advice he is giving and discuss these before watching how he helps his audience imitate the text. **Handout 6** includes this model text but, as Pie says, don't look at it while he is showing how to imitate it. At **57:22**, you can see that Pie has chosen to use a roll of wallpaper lining paper to draw his text map rather than several sheets of flipchart paper. You may want to ask your audience to follow the process with Pie. In which case, display a similar map that you have drawn earlier and see if your audience has internalised the text. If they need a little more help, lead them in doing this until they have internalised the text. (Obviously, make sure you have practised this yourself first so you are fully prepared to lead your audience!) You might find it easier to get everyone involved if you ask your audience to stand.	

12: **Advice on how to help children imitate the model text**
 	
(4 minutes)
	Play this clip up until **1:10:30**, having asked your audience to list Pie's advice as they watch. Then flipchart up the advice and discuss why each bit is important, as this advice is crucial.
	
	The key points are
	
	- Choose a **short** model text (around 250 words)
	- Keep it **simple**
	  – Do not have an icon for every word
	  – Do not have an action for every word
	
	If the imitation of the text fails with younger pupils, then the unit will fail because it is essential that they have internalised the text if they are to then build on the pattern.
	
	Then show the rest of this clip and discuss if you have any groups for whom the sort of text mapping that shows the paragraphs and boxes up each sentence would be useful.	

64 CREATING STORYTELLERS AND WRITERS

	13: Examples of children storytelling (4 minutes)	You may want to show these two short clips of children telling stories from their story maps to illustrate the expertise and confidence that the approach can give children. Ideally, you will be able to replace them with clips from your own school.
	14: Why internalising text matters (3 minutes)	This clip is a useful overview of the importance of the imitation stage and how you help embed the model in the children's minds. You may want to use it to embed understanding of both of these points.
	15: Modelling how to text map and express a story (4 minutes)	In this clip, Pie demonstrates how to story map. Again the story used is in **Handout 6**, but it is not needed for this clip. It may be important to show this clip because some teachers try to come up with a symbol for every word and make their maps far too complicated. As Pie explains, simple is best. Ask the audience to jot down the advice and the key steps. At the end of the clip, flipchart the main points and discuss why they are important. In particular, stress the importance of bringing the text alive. Following that discussion, it might be useful to put the second paragraph (reproduced below) up on screen and see if everyone can quickly text map this paragraph and then retell their paragraph to their neighbour, just using their map. *At that moment, Zelda sensed something crawling, something creeping along the pavement, hugging close to the shadows. Silently, a vague shape slipped into a doorway and Zelda was sure that she had glimpsed the flicker of a green eye. She could just hear a low growl even though the rain danced a thousand deaths on the pavement. Her fur prickled as she tensed herself. What was it?*
	16: The importance of teaching connectives and related actions (3 minutes)	This clip entertainingly illustrates the centrality of connectives to coherent text. Once your audience has listened to the clip, you may want to discuss • why connective phrases are important • how you are going to divide up the key connectives between years so that, year on year, the children's ability to write coherently progresses. • what activities will be good to warm up and embed connective phrases • how you are going to build progression across the years

APPENDIX 1   65

		It would be useful to provide your audience with copies of **Handouts 7 and 8** to support this session. **Handout 7** shows Pie's suggested actions for the key sentence signposts while **Handout 8** is an overview of how to link text effectively. It explains the different functions of conjunctions as opposed to adverbials and how this can alter the punctuation that a sentence needs. Since both terms are covered by the umbrella term connectives, some teachers confuse the two, so this article is helpful.
	17: Independent oral retelling (1 minute)	This short clip begins by summing up the difference between participation and communal retelling before focusing on independent retelling. This is a very useful technique for more confident storytellers in younger classes or for older classes who have already internalised basic story patterns. You may want to ask everyone to look back at the text map they did for the second paragraph of Zelda Claw, if you did that activity, and see if they can use it this time to retell that section of the story in their own words, embellishing it as they go.
	Clip 18: Introducing the written version of the text (1 minute)	This short clip is a useful overview of the imitation stage so far. It also emphasises how internalising the text allows everyone to have access to the written text once it is made available.
DVD 2: Imitation stage continued		
Reading as a reader		
	19: Reading as a reader – vocabulary (4 minutes)	Given the increasing difficulty of the SATs reading test, this clip is a useful reminder to lose no opportunity for strengthening the breadth and depth of the children's vocabulary. Pie refers to a number of vocabulary activities related to model text. Ask the audience to jot these down and pause the clip at **01:00** and flipchart these points and discuss them. Ask your audience to add in any other ways they have found of using model text to extend vocabulary.

		You may also want to pause at **01:09**, when the text beginning *Outside, the wind howled ...* is on screen (see **Handout 6**), and ask your audience to identify the words and phrases they think may need explaining. Then restart the clip so the audience hears Pie commenting on how idioms are often problematic. The clip ends by returning to some key strategies for building vocabulary. Ask your audience to see what needs adding to the list you made earlier.
	20: Reading as a reader – comprehension (2 minutes)	This clip is a useful reminder about what sort of questions are worth asking. Ask your audience to note down key points and then pool your understanding. You should end up with a co-constructed list of the type of questions that are worth asking. Pie also suggests ways that this in-house training on the art of questioning could be extended by getting teachers to work in pairs looking at model text and deciding which questions are worth asking (questions that develop inference). You may want to implement this suggestion.
	21: Reading as a reader – improving comprehension through booktalk (24 minutes)	This is an important clip because it illustrates Aidan Chamber's booktalk technique that is invaluable for strengthening inference, and is fully explained in his excellent, short book *Tell Me*. Ask your audience to listen carefully to the questions Pie is asking his audience in relation to the picture from Anthony Brown's *The Tunnel* and pause at **7:02**, when the picture is on screen, so that your audience has had a chance to discuss the image and the questions Pie has asked before they hear what Pie's audience says. When you continue the clip, ask the audience to note down what the rules of booktalk are so that at **9:24** you can flipchart these up and discuss them before Pie starts demonstrating the technique.

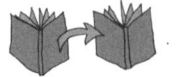

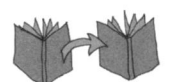

Before continuing the clip, you may want to ask someone, in role as TA, to flip chart the questions that Pie is asking and, at **10:45**, discuss why he has focused on such questions. During this section, you might also want to pause at some of the points when Pie asks a question so that your audience experiences the booktalk process. |

APPENDIX 1 67

| | You will notice that Pie never lets his audience know what he is thinking about the image – he just keeps on asking questions to open up thinking and facilitate the participation of the class. This is essential if booktalk is to work. It is worth asking your audience to listen very carefully to this section because Pie makes the booktalk process look deceptively simple but it is quite hard to do because you have to butt out of the conversation and this is alien to many teachers.

At **10:45**, Pie asks his audience what the main reading strategies were that they have been using and how did he do it. You may want to pause here and ask your audience the same questions before they listen to Pie's answers.

At **17:33**, Pie moves from using booktalk with a picture to using it with a text. Ask the audience to think about whether the underlying principles and the questions asked are basically the same. Coming to the conclusion that they are will help people reflect on the process.

At **17:56**, Pie asks his audience, 'What can you say about this?' Pause here and ask your audience the same question before listening to how Pie's audience responds.

At **20:57**, Pie asks his audience, 'Do you know what I think?' Pause and ask your audience if they know what Pie thinks, before listening to what he says to his audience about this.

The clip ends with some interesting reflections by Pie on the differences between the present National Curriculum and the previous one. |
| **22: Reading as a reader – overview of strategies** (2 minutes) | This clip begins with a useful range of active comprehension strategies. Again, you might want the audience to jot-down Pie's suggestions and pause at **24:02** to discuss them.

Then continue with Pie's overview of comprehension strategies. You may want to stress Pie's final point in this clip about providing a broader range of models to give the children a wider frame of reference. |

Reading as a writer

23: Reading as a writer – boxing up

(11 minutes)

Here Pie explains how reading as a writer is the bridge into the children having a go at doing similar writing themselves. He begins by explaining boxing up. **Handouts 5a and 5b** are a useful accompaniment to this clip as they illustrate how the structure of the key range of story types can be boxed up to help the children understand their underpinning structure. The first handout is for KS1 and the second for KS2 to show how understanding of the underpinning structure of stories should progress as the children get older.

Boxing up text is a simple but very powerful strategy for helping children understand the structure of a model text so they can apply a similar structure when they write themselves.

At **26:24,** you may want to pause and ask your audience to think about the advantages of planning the English curriculum around the underlying story patterns that Pie suggests (warning/journey/portal/wishing/character change, and lost and found stories) and how these can be built up across the years to provide children with the structure to create their own stories. He is suggesting this as the underpinning structure for curriculum planning and you may wish to discuss this. **Handouts 2a and 2b** will be useful here as they provide examples of this planning in practice.

Pause at **30:42** and provide your audience with a copy of **Handout 6** and ask them to look at *The Canal* and see if they can box up its structure using one box for each paragraph. Then watch the video to see how Pie does this.

At **33:18**, you may want to pause again and see if your audience can box up *Zelda Claw* (*see* **Handout 6**) before Pie shows them how to do it. Teaching boxing up clearly to classes is key to the children learning how to plan effectively so training time spent on this is time well spent.

●	**24: Reading as a writer – co-constructing the writing toolkit**
	
	(12 minutes)
		The opening of this clip is a useful addition to discussions about planning and building in progression. It shows how to help children build up toolkits for the 6 key features that underpin fiction writing: openings and endings, settings, suspense, characterisation, dialogue and description. Co-constructing these toolkits of writerly techniques relies on the teacher being able to help the children recognise the features and describe them in child-friendly language and this takes practice.
		
		Pause at **38:5** and see if your audience can identify a few of the writing tools that have been used in the extract from *The Canal* before Pie starts to explain them. Pie refers here to spine poems that had been covered in an earlier conference session. These will be included in a book on short-burst writing to accompany this fiction book (available in 2018). It would be useful to flipchart up the writing tools as Pie introduces them to help your audience reflect on what he is saying, just as Julia is flip-charting the toolkit as Pie says it.
		
		Your toolkit may end up looking something like this:
		
		Suspense toolkit
		To add suspense to a setting you could:
		- Select a good **adverb** to suggest danger: ***Cautiously**, they peered …*
		- Use a sentence of 3 to build up description: *The water was still, dark and deep*
		- Choose words carefully to make it sound scary – which adjectives would help?
		  - Put your main character in a dark place
		  - Stillness and silence suggest a threat – something's going to occur
		- Show the setting through the characters' eyes – *By the bank, they could see …*
		- Use **prepositions** to show the different places in the setting: ***By** the bank*
		- Use one or two short punchy sentences: *In the reeds, something rustled*.
		
		When co-constructing toolkits with a class, remember to begin with the writerly effect, followed by an example from the model. Avoid lists of grammatical features but use the technical terms when they are useful.

		The clip ends with a summary of how children become increasingly skilled at identifying toolkit features.
		Once your audience is familiar with the concept of co-constructing toolkits, introduce them to the importance of building in progression in these toolkits year on year. **Appendix 2** is a very useful resource designed to help you do this. Not only does it include what the toolkits might look like for each of the key 6 features but it also has a list of ideas for teaching this feature to different age groups so progression can be built in across the years. As Pie emphasises, over time, these toolkit should become internalised into a flexible toolkit in the children's heads that can be adapted to suit the audience, purpose and form of whatever type of writing they are doing.
	25: Making the learning visible (1 minute)	This brief clip focuses on the importance of capturing the key learning points and making them visible. You may want to use this clip to help establish the routine within your school. The washing line in each room should immediately show you what the learning focus is and it is useful for all subjects that are taught not just English.
Chapter 3: Innovation stage		
	26: Shared planning (simple substitution for early years) (5 minutes)	This introduction to the innovation stage begins by illustrating how to use Post-it notes to make simple substitutions on a text map. You may want to ask your audience to jot down all the key tips Pie gives and pause at the end of the clip (**53:46**) to discuss these; flip charting them helps embed the process for your audience, just as it does for the children, because it makes the learning visible.
		You may want to discuss how Pie waits for people to suggest the ideas that he has planned to use – or in extremis pretends someone has suggested it – to ensure the innovation covers the language features that he wants it to do. It is an entertaining moment but the underpinning logic of what he is doing is very important: planning your shared writing is key; if you follow every suggestion made by the children, your shared writing will lack focus.
		You may also want to ask your audience to reflect on why they should work on the oral retelling before they move to the writing.

💿	**27: Shared planning (boxing up the plan and talking the new text)** (6 minutes)	This clip shows how the same process works with older children. It is very important to move away from Post-it notes and simple substitution to boxing up because this facilitates much more adventurous innovation and encourages the class to increasingly move away from the model. Note how the audience's suggestions are added to the boxed-up planner on the flip-chart so the key elements of the plan are listed down. Also note that the planning should be brief and broad brush. Again, the children are asked to retell the new story from their plan. You may find it helpful to box up a new plan with your audience and then ask them to have a go at retelling the new version so they build up confidence in modelling this for a class. This process will help the children gain confidence as writers as they will have rehearsed what they are going to write before they write it. Pie then takes the audience through a boxed-up plan that was developed with a class and asks his audience to discuss this approach. Once you have shown this section of the clip, you may want to ask your audience the same question.
💿	**28: Shared writing illustrating hugging closely** (4.5 minutes)	Effective shared writing is key to the children making progress. For this reason, there are several clips on shared writing included in this DVD moving from simple to sophisticated. This first clip is all about how to hug closely to the model with groups that need a lot of support. You may want to pause at **1:00:35** and ask your audience to jot down all the advice that Pie gives on how to hug closely and then discuss this at the end of the clip, alongside considering which groups they might want to use this approach with. You may also want to discuss Pie's suggestion of training the TAs to do this.
💿	**29: More advanced shared writing** (9 minutes)	This shows Pie doing much more advanced shared writing with a year 6 class. It may be useful when watching this to provide your audience with copies of **Handouts 9 & 10**. While they are watching Pie illustrate shared writing, you may want to ask the TAs in your audience to jot down on **Handout 9** any additional useful phrases that Pie uses. At the same time, ask the teachers to see how many of the techniques listed on **Handout 10:** ***The art of shared writing*** Pie demonstrates in this clip. Following feedback from both groups, you may want to ask the teachers to reflect on how many of the techniques on **Handout 10** they use and whether they use them well.

| | | You may also want to arrange for all the teachers to be filmed doing shared writing so they can reflect on how well they do it and which areas might need improving.

You might also want to draw attention to
- Pie breaking in to praise a pupil for trying hard.
- The fact that Pie, with the little ones, was focusing on words but with the older pupils he is focusing on clauses or whole sentences because in years 5 & 6 that's what the children should be focusing on
- Pie's moment of panic when he thinks, *Is it a clause?* This is why preparation for shared writing is so important so that you are confident that what you are illustrating is both useful and accurate. |
|---|---|---|
| | **30: Planning a week's shared, guided and independent writing and editing**

(8 minutes) | This is a very practical clip where Pie takes the audience through how to plan a week's shared writing supported by guided writing, the opportunity for the children to write unaided and editing. Once your audience has watched this clip, you might want to ask them to do a similar piece of planning for the class that they teach so that this starts to become integrated into their practice.

You might also want to consider your marking policy in the light of Pie's comments and amend it if necessary to make it simple along the lines that Pie suggests. At **1:20:17**, Pie refers to Tim Roach, when teaching at Burnley Brow School, Oldham. |
| | **31: Different levels of innovation to move towards real independence**

(8 minutes) | This clip is well worth focusing on in its own right if, in your school, you feel that the shared writing is not sufficiently leading towards quality independent writing that has moved a long way away from the model. If your school is just starting out on the Talk for Writing approach, for shared writing it might be best to begin with **clips 28 & 29** and then use this clip as part of your follow-up training so that teachers become skilled at the hierarchy of shared writing as outlined by Pie.

Pie takes his audience through a range of ways of innovating on *The Canal* moving from hugging closely through simple addition to sophisticated addition, as well as flashback and sequel. Provide your audience with a copy of **Handout 12** so they can clearly see how the shared writing is being developed. |

| | | You may then want to provide your audience with a short model text like the one below and divide your audience up into pairs, according to the age-group they teach, with each pair focusing on a different level of shared writing innovation. The pairs could then discuss which features their shared writing was developing before pooling all the efforts and, hopefully, being able to see the progression in the writing. Practice at preparing thoroughly for shared writing, knowing exactly the type of sentences and language features you are modeling, will pay off.

Outside, the wind howled across fens. Inside, the school was dark. Sally tiptoed down the corridor, slipped into the classroom and began to search for the map.
At that moment, the wind fell silent. Sally heard the door creak open. She ducked down behind the table, her heart thudding and her mind ablaze with questions. Silently, somebody came into the classroom. A red eye flickered. Who was it?

This clip ends with a useful summary of how progression in shared writing over the years, supported by the washing line, can help children develop their writing skills. You may want to pause at **1:29:04** and ask your audience how the shared writing process supported by the washing line might help children progress before they hear Pie's explanation – and then play the end of the clip. |
|---|---|---|
| | **32: Two year 5 boys from Selby Community Primary School discussing writing** (4 minutes) | This clip of two year 5 boys from Selby Community Primary School is a useful reminder to teachers of how good teaching can lead to a real enthusiasm for language. The boy on the right had only been in this country for 2 years when this clip was filmed. Before showing this clip, ask your audience (when they watch it) to think about what they can tell about how these children have been taught. Discuss their conclusions at the end of the clip.

You may end up with a list like this:
The children
- Understand what effective verbs and adverbs are
- Understand the idea of hooking the reader
- Have been taught to extend their vocabulary
- Can explain a whole range of vocabulary activities: *dictionary deception; word waiters,* etc |

		• Confidently use grammatical terminology appropriately • Can explain *OSIE grids* coherently • Know that writing has to have an impact
	33: Overview of moving into writing, with a focus on marking (3 minutes)	This clip begins as a useful way of embedding the understanding begun by **Clip 30** of how to plan effective innovation. Pie then focuses on two-colour marking. This clip will be particularly useful if you want to introduce or embed this approach which is a simple and effective way of marking that is based on formative assessment research into what works. You may want to ask your audience to consider the advantages of two-colour marking and then discuss this at the end of this clip before showing **Clip 34**. **Handout 11** might be a useful addition here as it shows the sort of phrases teachers could model for the children to support self assessment – helping the children to think and talk in a writerly way and use grammatical terms constructively. These sorts of phrases are also very useful for the year 6 reading test.
	34: Making the marking lead to editing (2 minutes)	Now show this clip demonstrating the approach in more detail and, afterwards, continue the discussion. It clearly underlines that if the marking doesn't lead to the children editing their work, you are wasting your time. **Handout 4** on formative assessment is a useful document to circulate before watching **Clips 33 and 34** to help understand the action research that has gone into this approach.
Chapter 4: Independent application		
	35: Independent application (2 minutes)	As explained on page 44, the terminology that we use for explaining the Talk for Writing process has developed over the years. When this clip was filmed, we still called the Independent application stage *Invention*. We have adapted the terminology to be more accurate because, at this stage, the children are being asked to show that they can independently apply all the skills that they have focused on throughout the unit. Real creativity and invention comes when they have a free choice of what to write about in the way that they choose to write about it – see **Clip 36** and **Chapter 5**, page 52.

	Ask your audience, while watching this clip, to think about why the hot-task process is a useful way to end a unit of work and discuss this at the end of the clip. Hopefully, the discussion will bring out the importance of having a process that enables the pupils to reflect on their learning by comparing their initial cold task to the final hot task. This was also illustrated by **Clip 3** which showed how the approach bookends units. You may want to show this clip here. You may also want to stress the way in which Pie explains the need to plan what additional teaching may be needed to set up the independent application writing stage so all the children can succeed. Pie also points out that some schools leave the actual hot write, where the pupils show what they know, for a few weeks after the end of the unit so they can really assess if the learning has been internalised. You may want to discuss this idea.
Chapter 5: Achieving real independence through creativity and invention	
36: Opportunities for free creative writing (I minute)	Pie then goes on to explain the need to provide children, in between formal taught units, with real opportunities for invention. Interestingly, before the arrival of the literacy strategy in 1998, it was felt that children were spending too much time just being asked to write without being taught how to write. Now, perhaps, the pendulum has swung too far in the opposite direction and all writing is controlled: hence Pie's suggestion to rectify the balance and allow some time to promote free inventive writing and pupil choice so that they can achieve real independence. Before discussing this suggestion, draw your audience's attention to **Handouts 2a & 2b** that provide an overview of planning including this feature.
Conclusion	
37: Summary of the Talk for Writing process (1.5 minutes)	The final clip shows Pie summarising the Talk for Writing process from the flip charts that Julia produced in role as TA as he was explaining the process to his audience. **Handout 1** illustrates this process and will have been a useful handout to accompany viewing any clips from these DVDs as well as supporting this final clip.

Appendix 2: Toolkits for the 6 key story features

This resource should be of great value to teachers in helping their children write effectively. As emphasised throughout this book, the quality of the children's writing will be significantly enhanced if they understand the writerly tricks or tools, as we call them, that help a writer create a powerful effect on the reader. Not only does this resource show what the toolkits might look like for each of the key 6 writing features below, but it also has a list of ideas for teaching this feature to different age groups so progression can be built in across the years.

The writing tools need to be co-constructed progressively with classes so that understanding is developed as the children grow older and become more experienced readers and writers. Through practice, they will become embedded in the children's automatic understanding of how to write. By the end of year 6, the toolkits should no longer need to be displayed because the children have internalised them and can select the tools that they choose as they write in their own individual way to suit audience and purpose.

Anyone writing a story will need to have mastered the art of writing the following underpinning story features:

- Settings
- Suspense
- Characterisation
- Dialogue
- Description
- Openings and endings

The following toolkits have broken down the tools into what should be taught to the different age groups, and ways in which you might do this, so that the children can build up their skills of how to write these features effectively.

Settings toolkit

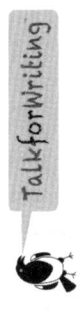

© Pie Corbett, 2017

To create a setting that the reader can imagine, which sounds real and has an atmosphere you might want to:

N/R	Y1/2 As in N/R plus:	Y3/4 As in Y1/2 plus:	Y5/6 As in Y3/4 plus:
• Draw maps showing different settings	• Choose a name for the setting	• Choose an interesting name for the setting	• Choose a name that suggests something about the setting, e.g. *Hangman's Wood*
• Create a simple story that starts and ends in the same place	• Try to 'see' it in your mind and use all senses to describe	• Select the time of day and weather to create an effect, e.g. *thunder rumbled through the darkness*	• Show the scene through the character's eyes – *Jill peered round the shop.*
• Create a simple story in which a main character goes from setting to setting on a journey	• Use sentences of 3 to describe	• Show how a character reacts to the setting: *Jo shivered.*	• Use a detailed sentence of 3 to describe what can be seen, heard or touched, e.g. *Old carpets, dusty sheets and broken chairs littered the floor.*
• Write a story with a local setting	• Take your character home to end the story	• Show the setting through the character's eyes, e.g. *Jo looked round the room.*	• Pick out unusual details to bring the setting alive, e.g. *On the piano, stood a large cage containing a yellow snake.*
• Select from a bank of photos or images of settings to help you	• Include some detail to bring a setting alive	• Use prepositions – *below the hill; near the cave; on top of the table*	• Introduce something unusual to hook the reader and lead the story forwards, e.g. *There was a letter on the doormat.*
• Choose a scary setting where something might happen, e.g. *bridge, forest, old house;*	• Choose adjectives with care; use 'like' and 'as' similes	• Use a change of setting, weather or time to create a new atmosphere.	• Change atmosphere by altering weather, place or time and use metaphor and personification, e.g. *the wind moaned*
• Use adjectives (*dark, gloomy, sunny*) and similes to describe settings (*it was dark as coal*)	• Include time of day and weather (*it was a hot night*)		• Reflect a character's feelings in the setting, e.g. *The rain poured and Gary sniffed.*
	• Select scary settings for dilemmas		

Useful ideas for teaching settings – always co-construct the toolkit with the class

Talk for Writing

Model all aspects of the toolkit and display word banks, sentences and ideas on prompt cards, washing lines or learning walls

N/R	Y1/2 As in N/R plus:	Y3/4 As in Y1/2 plus:	Y5/6 As in Y3/4 plus:
• Collect, display and use images of settings, e.g. *castle, forest, lake*; raid picture books & fairy tales	Collect banks of settings, weather & time of the day words for use	Collect language banks for settings, weather and time – sort by mood	Use images to train observation, brainstorm language and ideas. Shape these into descriptive passages
• Collect scary settings where something might happen, e.g. *bridge, forest, old house*	Collect banks of adjectives, powerful verbs and similes to build descriptions	Raid novels for images, descriptive passages and write 'in the style of'	From novels, collect and compare different settings that create different moods; write similar descriptions, shifting mood
• Use images of places and describe these, imagining a story happening. Compose simple captions	Use art work and real places for drawing and collecting descriptions	Compare descriptions and analyse effect created	Use film clips to discuss how settings manipulate the reader; write short descriptions of scenes
• Provide maps with different settings drawn or blank spaces for children to draw in settings	Use short-burst writing/ spine poems to teach description	Use drama to enter settings and mime how a character reacts	Use drama to create and describe settings; show an image/film clip and interview 'eye witnesses'; use guided visualisation to imagine scenes, e.g. *The Highwayman*
• Provide story floor mats and settings to choose from during story play, e.g. *toy trees, a garage*	Use drama to enter imagined worlds; move through different settings and describe	Use film and real locations for short-burst writing to develop description	Use physical theatre to build settings or retell tales; create still images and use 'talking objects' to describe
• Dramatise to help children imagine being in different settings and describing them	Use drama/ images to list words or invent sentences – what can you see, touch, smell and hear in the setting?	Use 'tell me' to develop settings through an imagined character's eyes	Use sound effects, music and voices to create and dramatise settings
• Re-enact a story with children becoming the scene, e.g. *a bridge*		Use 'in a dark, dark house' to build settings	

© Pie Corbett, 2017: This resource may be reprinted to support in-school training but should not be forwarded to others or used for commercial gain.

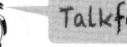

Suspense toolkit

© Pie Corbett, 2017

TalkforWriting

To create suspense to build tension, scare the reader and keep the reader wanting to find out what will happen you might want to:

N/R	Y1/2 As in N/R plus:	Y3/4 As in Y1/2 plus:	Y5/6 As in Y3/4 plus:

• put the main character into a scary setting – *forest, old bridge, empty house*
 	
• make the main character hear or see something
 	
• describe the threat
 	
• make the main character escape!
	• isolate your character/s
	  ○ in darkness/cold
	  ○ in a derelict setting
	
	• use scary sound effects, e.g. *something hissed*
	  ○ or show a glimpse, e.g. *a hand appeared ...*
	
	• show your character's reaction, e.g. *she shivered*
	
	• use exclamations to show impact
	
	• use dramatic connectives to introduce suspense and drama – *at that moment, suddenly, unfortunately*
		• let the threat get closer and closer
		
		• show the character's feelings by reactions, e.g. *she froze*
		
		• include short punchy sentences for drama
		
		• use rhetorical questions to make the reader worried – *Who had turned out the light?*
		
		• use empty words to hide the threat – *something, somebody, it, a silhouette*
		
		• select powerful verbs – *crept, grabbed, smothered*
		
		• use dramatic connectives – *in an instant, without warning, out of the blue*
			• hide the threat;
			
			• use an abandoned setting or lull the reader with a cosy setting
			
			• personify the setting to make it sound dangerous – use the weather and/or time of day to create atmosphere
			
			• make your character hear, see, touch, smell or sense something ominous
			
			• surprise the reader with the unexpected
			
			• suggest something is about to happen
			
			• reveal the character's thoughts, e.g. *She wondered if she would ever escape the darkness.*
			
			• slow the action by using sentences of three and drop in clauses.

Useful ideas for teaching suspense — always co-construct the toolkit with the class

Talk for Writing

Model all aspects of the toolkit and display word banks, sentences and ideas on prompt cards, washing lines or learning walls

N/R	Y1/2 As in N/R plus:	Y3/4 As in Y1/2 plus:	Y5/6 As in Y3/4 plus:
• Collect, display and use images of scary settings, e.g. *castle, bridge, forest, lake, old house* • Raid picture books & fairy tales for scary settings and notice descriptions • Use pictures and photos of scary places and describe these • Imagine a story happening with a scary moment • Compose simple descriptive captions and sentences • Dramatise and imagine being in a scary setting, showing reactions	• Read stories with suspense – innovate on sentences • Dramatise stories where main character hears or sees something scary • Show main character's reactions • Collect words to describe a character's reaction and use in sentences, e.g. *froze, hid, ducked down, trembled, shivered* • Rehearse sentences using dramatic connectives to introduce a sound effect or glimpse, e.g. *At that moment, she heard… / At that moment, she saw* • Show images of scary places and list what might happen	• Collect language banks for scary settings, ominous weather, cold and darkness – sort by mood • Raid novels for scary scenes, descriptive passages and write 'in the style of' • Compare suspense sections and analyse effect created • Use drama to recreate suspense, mime how a character reacts and hot seat • Use 'in a dark, dark house' to build suspense • Collect verbs, dramatic connectives, empty words, descriptive phrases to use when building suspense	• From novels, collect and compare different suspense paragraphs and innovate • Use film clips to discuss how to manipulate the reader; write short suspense scenes • Use drama to create a suspense scene • Use sound effects, music and voices to create suspense • Hot seat characters from drama and a novel to explore feelings and thoughts at moments of suspense – turn into writing • Gather word banks for suspense using the senses • Rehearse suspense sentences using sentences of three to build tension and drop in clauses; contrast with rhetorical questions and short sentences

© Pie Corbett, 2017: This resource may be reprinted to support in-school training but should not be forwarded to others or used for commercial gain.

Characterisation toolkit

To create characters that sound real and the reader can imagine you might want to:

N/R	Y1/2 As in N/R plus:	Y3/4 As in Y1/2 plus:	Y5/6 As in Y3/4 plus:

• Write about a character from a story you know or make up a new character
 	
• Give your character a name
 	
• Use adjectives to describe e.g. *friendly, scary* and use a simile – using *like* or *as* e.g *with wrinkles like a walnut*
 	
• Have a 'goodie' and a 'baddie'
 	
• Give your character a problem
 	
• End with 'happily ever after'
	• Use simple similes to describe e.g. *He stood as tall as a tree*
	
	• Use sentence or power of 3 e.g. *Santa was red, fat and friendly.*
	
	• Use adverbs to describe how something does something e.g. *she tiptoed quietly*
	
	• Use adjectives to describe a noun with a comma (simple noun phrases), e.g. *a small, round ball*
	
	• Introduce bits of alliteration e.g. *Sally slept silently*
		• Show not tell – describe a character's emotions using senses, e.g. the effect on the character's body –. *a shiver shot up her spine*
		
		• Give your main character a hobby, interest or special talent:
		  - *Shiv kept a pet rat called Simon in a cage made of bamboo shoots*
		  - an expression for speech, e.g. '*Rats!*' *she cried*
		  - something they love or hate or fear, e.g. *Carol had always been afraid of the dark*
		  - a distinctive feature, e.g. *she wore scarlet jeans*
		  - a secret
		
		• Know your character's desire, wish or fear, e.g. *Gareth had always wanted a pet/ never liked lizards.*
			• Use a name to suggest the character, e.g. *Mr Hardy* [strong and tough], *Miss Honey* [gentle]
			
			• Drop in a few details to suggest character, e.g. *Mr Simons, gripping his cane, glared at the two boys.*
			
			• Show (not tell) how characters feel by what they do, think or say, e.g. "*Get out!*" *he snapped, slamming the door.* (to show anger)
			
			• Reveal a character's thoughts, e.g. *He hoped that he would find his way home.*
			
			• Use other character's (or the narrator's comments or reactions, e.g. '*Tracy's upset again,*' *whispered Jamil.*
			
			• Use contrasting main characters & show how a character feels on the inside whilst pretending something else.
			
			• Show character development – how they feel at the start and end of a story, e.g. *Mrs Bonny frowned.* [Opening] *Mrs Bonny turned to her new-found friend and smiled.* [Ending]

© Pie Corbett, 2017

Talk for writing

Useful ideas for teaching characterisation – always co-construct the toolkit with the class

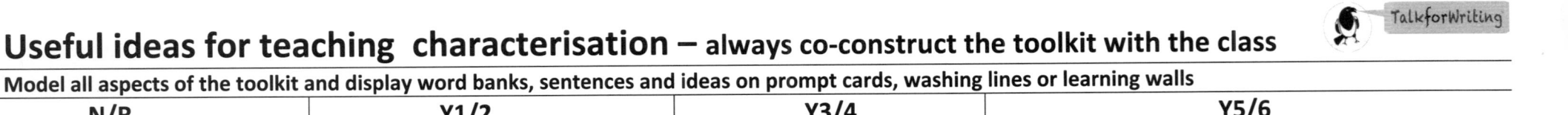

Model all aspects of the toolkit and display word banks, sentences and ideas on prompt cards, washing lines or learning walls

N/R	Y1/2 As in N/R plus:	Y3/4 As in Y1/2 plus:	Y5/6 As in Y3/4 plus:
• Collect a bank of characters from reading	• From reading, create 'role on the wall', collecting character clues and tracking development	• Notice and collect ideas for how authors develop characters through what they say, do and thin	• Play games where children mime and others have to guess – who and how they feel
• Notice, collect and use descriptive language	• Add speech or thought bubbles to pictures	• Use reading and images to collect banks of words or phrases to draw on when writing for feelings, e.g. *scared – shivered, spine tingle, legs shook, tremble*	• Write dialogue for images of films with the sound turned down
• Ask class to sort characters into goodies and baddies	• Collect, display and use a bank of descriptive language (adjectives & similes)		• Collect banks of names and idioms/expressions
• Discuss how characters feel and find clues in the text or images	• Use drama/ mime/ play 'in the manner of the word' to show how a character feels, e.g. *walked sadly*	• act out simple scenes with different characters, e.g. *coming into a room angrily, shyly, bossily, etc.*	• Look at images of people and write banks of details to describe faces, hands, eyes, mouths, teeth, etc.
• Discuss dilemmas for characters	• Create banks of words to describe how a character feels	• Use drama to re-enact or develop new scenes	• In reading, discuss how authors build characters and show/suggest feelings
• Role-play scenes in stories	• Draw characters + speech bubbles	• Collect character triggers, e.g. *a secret, a wish, a fear, finding something, an anxiety, a dream, losing something, a lie, etc.*	• Use drama to develop 'show not tell'. Act out scenes, changing a character's feelings, e.g. how does a bossy character answer the door or a shy one?
• Invent new characters together	• Role-play brief conversations before writing dialogue		• Rehearse changing sections of good writing by altering the character type thinking about what a different character would say, do or think;
• Use hats, costumes and puppets to retell or invent stories with strong central characters	• Use freeze frames, hot seat and interview characters		
• Draw characters on story map			• Read and imitate good writers. Borrow characters and write new stories for them.

© Pie Corbett, 2017: This resource may be reprinted to support in-school training but should not be forwarded to others or used for commercial gain.

Dialogue toolkit

Talk for Writing

To create dialogue that sounds real, reflects character and moves action forwards you might want to

N/R	Y1/2 As in N/R plus:	Y3/4 As in Y1/2 plus:	Y5/6 As in Y3/4 plus:
- Use puppets and make up funny voices when playing role-play different characters - Read aloud using different voices for characters - Discuss 'What did the character say?', 'why' and model 'How?' - On story maps, draw simple speech inside speech bubbles - Notice speech marks in shared reading; - When the sound is turned down in films, discuss what they might be saying - Use wordless picture books and discuss what a character might say.	- Choose and decide how a character feels, thinks or behaves and show this through what they say, *e.g. 'I'm scared!'* - Use powerful speech verbs – *hissed, squealed, roared, whispered* - Use said plus an adverb – *he said nervously* **And a few speech punctuation rules:** - Write what is said, starting with a capital letter, and the punctuation inside a speech bubble - Burst the bubble to leave speech marks round what is said - Start a new line for each speaker - Start the spoken words with a capital letter - If the sentence ends with speech, put a . or ! or ? inside the speech marks. If the sentence continues end the speech with a comma	- Use only a few exchanges - Tag on what a character is doing while speaking, using a 'stage direction' – *'No,' he hissed, <u>shaking his head.</u>* - Use a speech sandwich, e.g. *'Hello,' said John, waving to his friend. Then character B replies, 'Run for it', squealed Tim.* - Use dialogue to suggest how a character feels, thinks or what they are like and to move the action forwards - Use quirky expressions, e.g. *"Crazy cats," she muttered.*	- Have characters discuss other characters and reflect on events - Add to the speech sandwich by adding in the listener's reaction, e.g. *'Hello,' said John, waving to his friend. Tim gasped.* - Also add in something else that is needed to keep the action moving forwards, e.g. *'Hello,' said John, waving to his friend. Tim gasped. Coming down the road was an elephant.* - Complete with what the listener says, e.g. *'Hello,' said John, waving to his friend. Tim gasped. Coming down the road was an elephant. 'Run for it!' squealed Tim.* - Put the speaker before or after what is said or in between, e.g. *Sam said, "So, let's go."* *"So, let's go," said Sam.* *"So," said Sam, "Let's go."*

© Pie Corbett, 2017

Useful ideas for teaching dialogue – always co-construct the toolkit with the class

Talk for Writing

Model all aspects of the toolkit and display examples on washing lines.

N/R	Y1/2 As in N/R plus:	Y3/4 As in Y1/2 plus:	Y5/6 As in Y3/4 plus:
• Provide role-play spaces, costumes, hats and objects/toys to encourage role-play and re-enacting of stories • Provide puppets and play with children • Use picture books and big books – read aloud together with expression, emphasising who says what and how – discuss how characters feel and how we know • Read together using voices to match how a character feels • Discuss what character might be thinking and what they might do or say next • Use Post-its in Big Books or on screen to add in dialogue • Capture what children say on laminated speech bubbles & provide for play	• Focus on dialogue in reading and work out simple rules • Display dialogue rules and examples on washing lines and on support cards • Rehearse dialogue in shared writing but keep it limited • Draw cartoons with speech bubbles for stories • Practice turning speech bubbles into dialogue • Use Post-its to innovate on speech verbs, adding in adverbs or changing what is said • Change a character's personality and then alter what they say	• Add ideas to class dialogue rules by reading quality literature, display, model in shared writing and practise • Use paired drama to develop what is said and how it is said with expression mirroring how a character feels plus a simple action, e.g. *pointing at the chair* • Model in pairs what character A says + the reply from character B; then add in stage directions for both • Collect expressions from books but also from listening in to other people speaking • Make lists of idioms and everyday expressions	• Notice in reading how other characters or the author, reflect on a main character • In drama, use the game 'gossip' or 'spies' to develop the idea of other characters commenting on a key character • Identify in reading and model in shared writing how the listener reacts; use drama to explore how reactions can be 'shown'; • Explore dialogue in quality books and add extra ideas to the class dialogue rules and tips • Innovate on extracts of dialogue from novels, using same style as author • Innovate from novels by changing how a character feels, using 'show not tell' and altering what they say – can a partner guess how your character feels?

© Pie Corbett, 2017: This resource may be reprinted to support in-school training but should not be forwarded to others or used for commercial gain.

Description toolkit

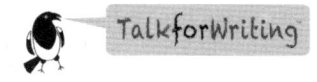

© Pie Corbett, 2017

TalkforWriting

To create a description that the reader can imagine, making it sound real and using it to intrigue, you might want to:

N/R	Y1/2 As in N/R plus:	Y3/4 As in Y1/2 plus:	Y5/6 As in Y3/4 plus:
• Look attentively and talk about new experiences • Use adjectives (describing words) to say what images and objects look like • Look carefully at images, objects, animals, events, etc. • Use all the senses to discuss and describe – look, touch, taste, hear and smell • Use powerful verbs to describe the quality of movement, e.g. 'crept' instead of 'tiptoed'	• Use precise nouns to 'name it' and create a picture in the reader's mind, e.g. *poodle* rather than *dog* • Choose adjectives with care and use a comma, e.g. *the small, round pot* • Sentence or power of 3 to describe, e.g. *Santa was red, fat and friendly.* • Choose powerful verbs rather than – *got, came, went, said, look* • Use adverbs to describe how something does something e.g. *she tiptoed quietly* • Experiment with alliteration • Use 'as' and 'like' similes • Observe carefully and draw on all the senses when describing.	• 'Show' not 'tell' – describe a character's emotions using senses or a setting to create an atmosphere. e.g. *The shadow darted forwards. Her skin crawled!* • Select powerful, precise and well-chosen nouns, adjectives, verbs, adverbs that really match e.g. *rusted, overgrown, smeared, smothered* • Use personification e.g. *the bushes seemed like they were holding their breath* • Use metaphors and similes to create atmosphere, e.g. *even the tables froze* • Use alliteration to add to the effect, e.g. *Sally slept silently. The dark, damp, dangerous wood...* • Use expanded noun phrases to add intriguing detail e.g. *The shaggy dog at the end of the lane begged on all fours.*	• Use a character's reaction or the author's comments to show the effect of a description, e.g. *Joanna shuddered.* • Use onomatopoeia rather than alliteration to reflect meaning, e.g. *The bees buzzed busily.* • Ensure all word choices earn their place and add something new and necessary, e.g. not *the red letterbox* but *the rusted letterbox* • Use precise detail when describing to bring a scene alive, e.g. *His gold fob watch glinted.* • Select detail and describe for a purpose, e.g. to scare the reader, to lull the reader.

Useful ideas for teaching description — always co-construct the toolkit with the class

Talk for Writing

Model all aspects of the toolkit and display word banks, sentences and ideas on prompt cards, washing lines or learning walls

N/R	Y1/2 As in N/R plus:	Y3/4 As in Y1/2 plus:	Y5/6 As in Y3/4 plus:
Use new experiences – images, objects, animals, places, characters – to discuss and 'say what it looks like';	Regular painting and drawing of objects, animals, scenes, etc.;	Teach drawing – close observational work;	Avoid overwriting when describing. Learn how to trim/ tighten sentences.
Develop the use of the 5 senses and related language through specific experiences, e.g. feely bag, curiosity corner, nature table, nature walks, etc.;	Develop use of 5 senses through science;	Develop language and observation through science work. Use lenses;	Avoid repeating ideas, telling the reader the obvious (*hot flames*) and only select description that adds something new and moves the plot forwards.
Carefully draw and paint set pieces;	Constant modeling of descriptive language by adults;	Regular new experiences to discuss and describe. Play descriptive barrier games;	Discuss how good authors balance description and action.
Guided discussion, focused on a stimulus with word gathering;	Train children to generate descriptive language and add to their word banks with new vocabulary;	Use short-burst 'spine' writing to practice observational writing;	Gather creative imagery into banks and discuss effects on the reader.
Constant modeling of descriptive language by adults.	Use collections to reinforce language, e.g. *shiny things, soft things, colour tables*, etc.;	Brainstorm banks of vocabulary, list and use when writing;	Map, learn and write in the style of the best descriptive passages available, e.g. description of the barn in *Charlotte's Web*.
	Collect interesting descriptive words and sentences from quality books and 'bank' for future use.	Use magpie books and boards to gather great descriptions from quality books.	Gather specific words banks through short-burst writing before writing narrative.
			Draw on previous writing and raid for effective imagery and description.

© Pie Corbett, 2017: This resource may be reprinted to support in-school training but should not be forwarded to others or used for commercial gain.

Openings and endings toolkit

© Pie Corbett, 2017 — TalkforWriting

To create openings and endings that hook the reader you might want to:

N/R	Y1/2 As in N/R plus:	Y3/4 As in Y1/2 plus:	Y5/6 As in Y3/4 plus:

• Learn a 'Once upon a time' opening
 	
• Learn 'Once upon a time there was a …' to establish a character in a setting. E.g. 'Once upon a time there was a pirate who lived on an island.'
 	
• Learn to end a story with 'Finally' or 'In the end' plus 'happily ever after'.
	• Think about how the character feels/ what the character wants before the story starts
	
	• Add more ways to start a story, using the 'time' starter 'one', e.g. One day; One morning; One afternoon; One night …
	
	• Add in 'early' or 'late', e.g. Late one night; Early one morning …
	
	• Use 'place' starters, e.g. In a distant land; Far, far away; On the other side of the mountain, etc.
	
	• Use more time starters, e.g. 'Once, not twice; Long ago; Many moons ago …'
	
	• End by stating how the character has changed or what has been learned, 'He would never steal again.' Or, take your characters home.
		• Use time (Late one night), weather (Snow fell) or place starters (The river teemed with fish) – 'who', 'where', 'when', 'weather' and 'what' (is happening) to orientate the reader
		
		• Start with the name of your character, e.g. 'Bill stared out of the window'. Think about how the character feels (or personality, e.g. bossy) and show this at the start, e.g. 'Bill glared at his teacher.'
		
		• Use dramatic speech – "How do we escape now?" (Try warnings, worries, dares, secrets.)
		
		• Start with questions or exclamations to hook the reader's interest, e.g. "Run!" they yelled./ "What is it?" she muttered.
		
		• End by showing how the character has changed, 'Bill grinned.' or what has been learned, e.g. a moral
			• 'Hook' the reader, e.g.
			  ○ Usually, Tim enjoyed playing in the park but …
			  ○ Use a contrast, e.g. inside/ outside: Outside, the wind howled. Inside, the fire blazed.
			  ○ Use a dilemma, desire or unexpected event, e.g. Jo wept.
			  ○ Suggest something dangerous might happen (the ancient bridge shook) or has happened (smoke rose from the village)
			  ○ Dismiss the 'monster', e.g. Tim had never believed in ghosts.
			  ○ Create a mood (The fog shrouded …)
			  ○ Use a 'trigger' to catch the reader's interest, e.g. someone wants something; is warned not to do something; has to go somewhere; is threatened; has lost something; a mysterious parcel arrives
			
			• Use a flashback or forwards.
			
			• End by showing what the main character has learned or how they have changed. Make a link back to the beginning. Have the author comment on events.

Useful ideas for teaching openings and endings – always co-construct the toolkit with the class

Model all aspects of the toolkit and display possible openings and endings on the washing line or working wall

N/R	Y1/2 As in N/R plus:	Y3/4 As in Y1/2 plus:	Y5/6 As in Y3/4 plus:
• Notice and use common openings and endings from well-loved picture books • Repeat common storytelling openings/ endings such as 'Once upon a time' or 'Finally, they …' in storytelling • Emphasise in storytelling the importance of the main character and where they lived • Use banks of familiar characters and settings to develop familiar opening patterns such as 'Once upon a time there was a … who lived ….'	• Hot seat, in role, as a main character at the start of a story – what do they feel/ desire, where do they live/ where are they going/ what are they doing – then turn into oral telling of the opening or shared writing • Repeat hot seating of the main character to develop the ending, focusing on how the character has changed or what has been learned • Notice, collect and try using openings from picture books and oral stories • Build up a bank of cards with time starters, characters, settings so that children can choose different ways to open/ end stories • Use objects, pictures, film clips, trips, visitors to trigger story beginnings	• Use drama to develop 'show not tell' to deepen openings and endings • Use role-play to develop possible 'speech' openings and translate with shared writing • Collect and categorise openings from story books, e.g. ones that start with speech, a character's name, the setting, a question, a dilemma, etc. • Discuss which openings hook the reader and what techniques are being used • Work on planning with a character, in a *place, the time of day and weather*. Then add in *'why the character is there'* and *'how the character feels'*	• Collect adverbials to hook the reader, e.g. *'Usually', 'amazingly', 'suddenly'* • Work from objects, images, experiences • Model how to tease the reader by leaving gaps and a back-history, e.g. *'Mrs Jenkins was not going to be fooled again.'* • Compare different openings/ endings by quality writers and discuss which is most powerful and why. Then contrast openings with their endings - look for links • Use shared and guided writing to model effective openings that hook the reader and endings that draw a story together. Reflect what has changed/ been learned • Experiment by writing various openings, thinking about the desired effect on the reader, e.g. to make them laugh, feel sad, want to read on, etc.

© Pie Corbett, 2017: This resource may be reprinted to support in-school training but should not be forwarded to others or used for commercial gain.

Handout 1

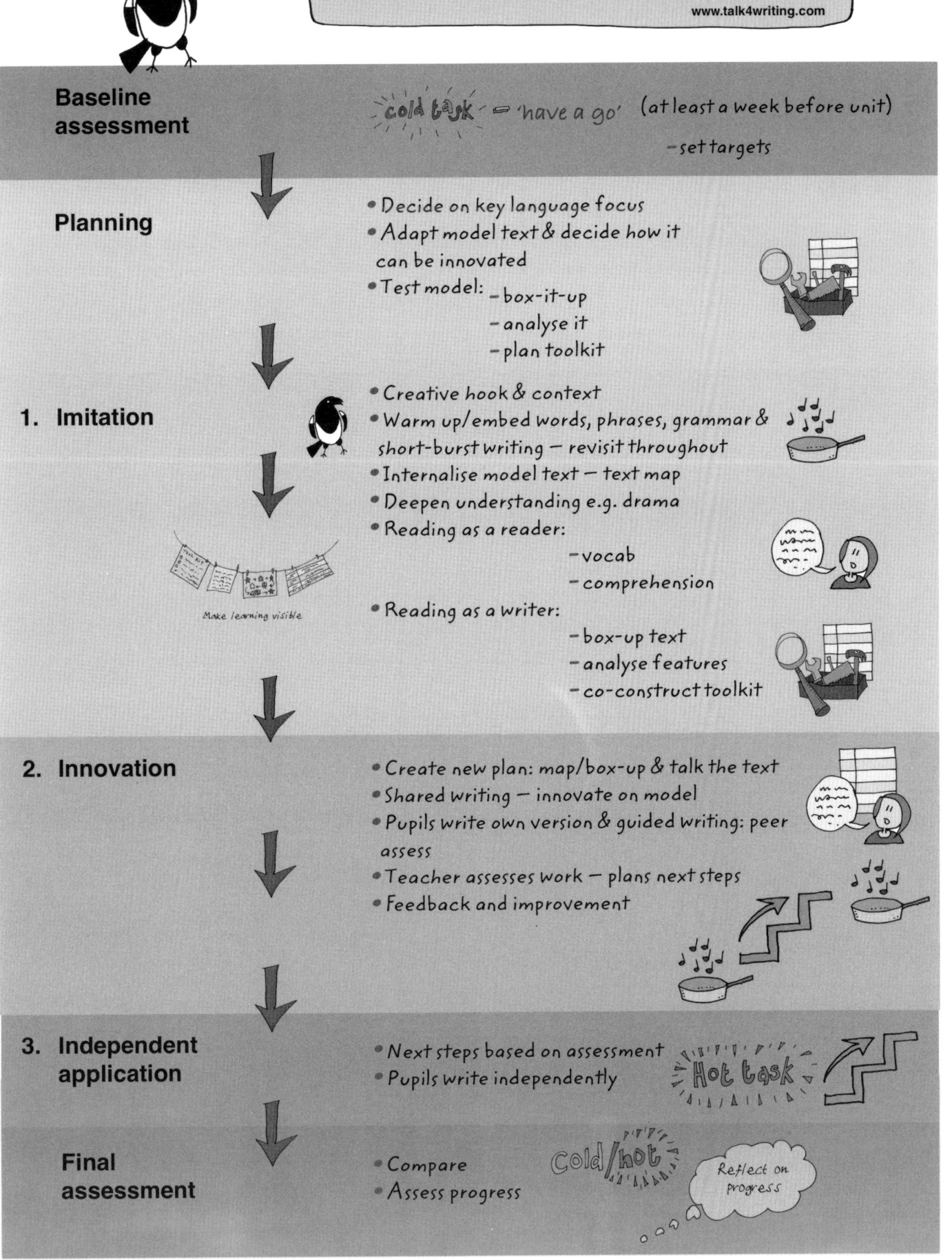

The Talk for Writing process
www.talk4writing.com

Baseline assessment
cold task – 'have a go' (at least a week before unit)
– set targets

Planning
- Decide on key language focus
- Adapt model text & decide how it can be innovated
- Test model:
  - box-it-up
  - analyse it
  - plan toolkit

1. Imitation
- Creative hook & context
- Warm up/embed words, phrases, grammar & short-burst writing – revisit throughout
- Internalise model text – text map
- Deepen understanding e.g. drama
- Reading as a reader:
  - vocab
  - comprehension
- Reading as a writer:
  - box-up text
  - analyse features
  - co-construct toolkit

Make learning visible

2. Innovation
- Create new plan: map/box-up & talk the text
- Shared writing – innovate on model
- Pupils write own version & guided writing: peer assess
- Teacher assesses work – plans next steps
- Feedback and improvement

3. Independent application
- Next steps based on assessment
- Pupils write independently

Hot task

Final assessment
- Compare
- Assess progress

cold/hot

Reflect on progress

© Pie Corbett & Julia Strong – Talk4Writing.com

This resource may be reprinted to support in-school training but should not be used for commercial gain.

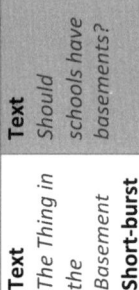

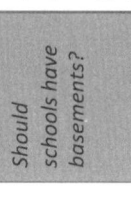

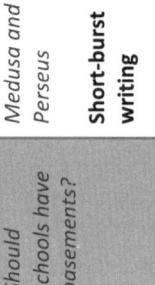

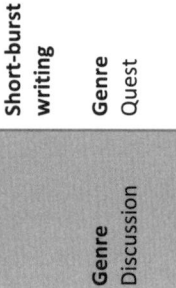

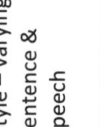

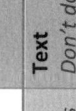

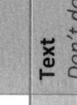

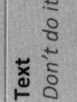

Talk for Writing

Overview of planning Years 3–4

Handout 2a

Insert free-writing week here (between each half-term block)

Year 3

	Autumn 1		Autumn 2		Spring 1		Spring 2		Summer 1		Summer 2	
	Fiction	Non-fiction	Fiction	Non-fiction	Fiction	Non-fiction	Fiction	Non-fiction	Fiction	Non-fiction	Fiction	Non-fiction
Text	3 Billy Goats Gruff	How to trap a troll	The Reluctant Dragon	Dragons	Adventures at Sandy Cove	The beach trip	Daft Jack	Invitation to Jack's wedding	The Thing in the Basement	Should schools have basements?	Medusa and Perseus	What you need to do to defeat Medusa
	Short-burst writing		Short-burst writing		Short-burst writing		Short-burst writing		Short-burst writing		Short-burst writing	
Genre	Wishing tale	Instructions	Defeating the monster tale	Information	Warning tale	Recount in form of a letter	Losing tale	Persuasion	Finding tale	Discussion	Quest	Explanation
Focus	Character		Setting		Action		Openings & endings		Suspense		Style – varying sentence & speech	

Year 4

	Fiction	Non-fiction	Fiction	Non-fiction	Fiction	Non-fiction	Fiction	Non-fiction	Fiction	Non-fiction	Fiction	Non-fiction
Text	The Fountain of Immortality	Should foxes be hunted	Cockleshell Heroes	How to blow up war ships	War horse	Our trip to London	Pandora's Box	Weather disasters	The Noise	How rock pools are formed	Risky Business	Don't do it!
	Short-burst writing		Short-burst writing		Short-burst writing		Short-burst writing		Short-burst writing		Short-burst writing	
Genre	Quest tale	Discussion	Defeating monster tale	Instruction	Tale of fear	Recount in form of a letter	Losing tale	Information	Finding tale	Explanation	Warning Tale	Persuasive
Focus	Setting		Character		Action		Description – people, places & objects		Suspense		Cliffhangers	

© Pie Corbett & Julia Strong: www.talk4writing.com   This resource may be reprinted to support in-school training but should not be forwarded to others or used for commercial gain.

Overview of planning Years 5 – 6

Handout 2b

Insert free-writing week here →

		Autumn 1		Autumn 2		Spring 1		Spring 2		Summer 1		Summer 2	
		Fiction	Non Fiction	Fiction	Non Fiction	Fiction	Non Fiction	Fiction	Non Fiction	Fiction	Non Fiction	Fiction	Non Fiction
Year 5	Text	*The Story of Isis and Osiris*	*Mummification – the truth!*	*The Lost*	*How to keep a dragon amused*	*Little Red Riding Hood*	*Should the wolf's name be cleared?*	*Why the Whales Came*	*Protect the whales*	*Harry Potter*	*Adverts & leaflets for Hogwarts School*	*Doctor Who*	*Daleks*
		Short-burst writing		Short-burst writing		Short-burst writing		Short-burst writing		Short-burst writing		Short-burst writing	
	Genre	Wishing tale	Explanation	Losing tale	Instructions	Quest tale	Discussion	Warning tale	Journalistic recount	Defeating the monster	Persuasion	Tale of fear	Information
	Focus	Character		Suspense		Setting		Characterisation / dialogue		Description		Action	
Year 6	Text	*Kidnapped*	*How to keep a dragon amused; News report; police interview*	*The Canal*	*Tom's diary; letters; how canals work; is play dangerous?*	*White Horse of Zennor*	*Unicorns; Morpurgo's life; persuasive letters*	*Holes*	*Should Stanley try to escape? Court report; letter home*	*Beowulf*	*Trap an ogre; monster reports; News bulletin; persuade a hero; should monster be saved? etc*	Focused invented writing covering all text types	Focused invented writing - 'Spies' theme – basic plot patterns and all non-fiction text types + daily short-burst writing
		Short-burst writing		Short-burst writing		Short-burst writing		Short-burst writing		Short-burst writing		Short-burst writing	
	Genre	Tale of Quest	Instructions / recount types	Tale of fear	Recount types; explanation; discussion	Wishing Tale	Information auto/biography; persuasion	Warning Tale	Discussion; formal writing; recount	Defeating the monster	all text types + mixed texts/ formal and informal		
	Focus	Suspense		Setting		Character		Action		Style/vocab			

© Pie Corbett & Julia Strong: www.talk4writing.com   This resource may be reprinted to support in-school training but should not be forwarded to others or used for commercial gain.

Handout 4   TalkforWriting

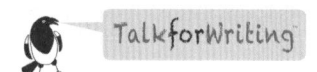

Formative assessment:
the key to progress

Context: create a positive mindset (see work of Carol Dweck)

> "Such labeling will stay with the children all their lives."

✔ Do praise effort & strategy – creates growth mindset

✘ Don't praise ability – creates fixed mindset
- I'm useless so I don't try.
- I'm good so I don't need to try.

"I am 2c."

Create a CAN-DO attitude. Don't label children with levels. *"We can all get better."*
The obsession with level (summative assessment) has led to the absolute contrary becoming commonplace. Many schools have ladders on the wall displaying which child is on what grade. Summative assessment has become a form of labeling and it lowers standards. Instead, it should only provide a way of measuring what children can do and facilitate comparing children's progress.

Formative assessment is at the heart of effective teaching, as research has unequivocally established (see Dylan Wiliam *The Black Box* or the *EEF toolkit* or the work of Shirley Clarke). Quality teaching guided by formative assessment can help everyone improve.
Formative assessment enables you to know what the children can do and to use that to establish what you need to teach next. It demands flexible planning: what happens on Monday, determines the focus of Tuesday etc.

"Every school needs a systematic approach to formative assessment."

✘ Don't allow the 'Marjorie syndrome' – where one or two teachers refuse to go along with the system.

✔ Create a learning culture based on formative assessment and apply this systematically. *"If you want to teach here, this is what you do because it will help the children learn."*

"Formative assessment combined with quality teaching and high expectations = effective teaching and learning."

How the 3 stages of the Talk for Writing approach puts formative assessment at the heart of your teaching

- **Imitation:** model text – learn text orally to internalise the language patterns
- **Innovation:** show the children how to innovate on the pattern through shared writing and then they write their own version
- **Invention application:** children can write this type of text on their own

Move from DEPENDENCE ————▶ to INDEPENDENCE

Set COLD task before begin unit

- Observe children as a writers – learning habits
- Use children's work to help you decide what features need to be focused on (mull over cold task/ seek advice of others to help focus teaching)
- Adapt the unit to fit the need:
    - Write/adapt model text to exemplify the features selected for whole class
    - Decide what additional features groups/individual children need

What happens on each day of a unit will affect how the next day is taught – therefore **planning must be flexible** so it can adapt to fit need.

"Have a go."

At end of Invention/Independent application stage, set a similar HOT task – Can the children use all the features that have been focused on?

"Show what you know."

Compare the cold and hot tasks so you can see the progress:
- Teacher can assess what needs to be focused on next;
- Children can discuss and log their progress and transfer skills;
- Teacher can assess the effectiveness of their teaching.

The logical flow from dependence to independence is based on the quality of the formative assessment that guided the teaching.

"Formative assessment should be happening all the time: it should underpin the direction of the teaching."

Imitation stage

The COLD task drives the teaching and the learning because it establishes the features to focus on. Observing the children's learning behaviours also helps you select the hook for the unit.

Adapt the model text (no more than 450 words) so that it exemplifies the features focused on to set the standard and build in progression.

"Show what you know."

- Someone in school needs to oversee the quality and progression of this exemplar text so that progression is built in from term to term and year to year.

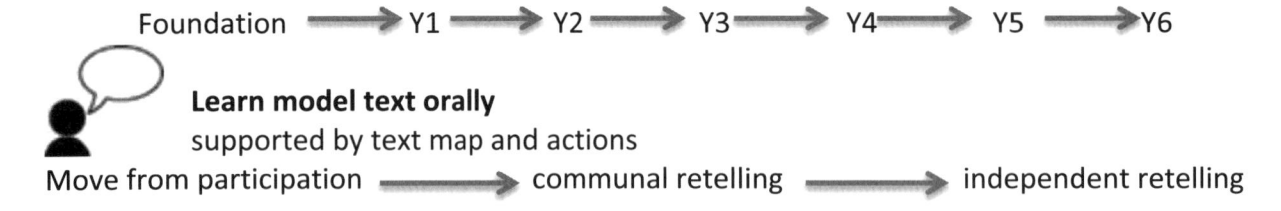

Foundation → Y1 → Y2 → Y3 → Y4 → Y5 → Y6

Learn model text orally
supported by text map and actions

Move from participation → communal retelling → independent retelling

Once the text is internalised, begin to analyse the text by:

- **Reading as a reader** – comprehension – to deepen understanding – extend through wider reading and examples
- **Reading as a writer** – begin to understand the underlying pattern of features

Underpinned and extended by:

- high expectations
- daily word and sentence activities focused on the key features which increasingly integrate grammatical understanding
- deepening understanding through wider examples:
- insisting on the children doing what they have been taught – sort errors systematically

"80% of vocabulary comes from reading."

"We set the standards:
– the barrier is in the teacher's head."

from imitation ⟶ innovation

- Devise activities to deepen understanding of
    - Comprehension of the text – **reading as a reader**
    - The pattern of language of text type being focused on – **reading as a writer**
        - The language features being focused on – daily word and sentence work

Reading as a writer – analyse the structure and language features:

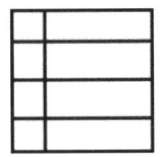

- Structure – Plan it
    - story mountains – ensure you build in progression
    - **Boxing up** – co-construct with the class how to identify the underlying structure of the text: each box represents a paragraph / section of the writing
- Key features 

Toolkits
- co-construct the ingredients so the children understand
- show the children how to choose which to use: *"What are the features that would help make this writing effective?"*
- Use everyday language about features so the children understand eg: *"Put main character in a dodgy setting"*

Beware of a plethora of reductive tick-list success criteria
- Involve the pupils by co-constructing the optional toolkit. The only "you must" criteria which could be ticked off are the fixed features of the basic writing rules (or everyday toolkit) eg

Basic writing toolkit
- Capital letters at beginning of sentences
- Full stops at the end of sentences
- Finger spaces between the words
- Write on the line

"Remember to encourage the children to read their work aloud and see if it works."

Innovation stage

- Use formative assessment to decide what level of innovation in the shared writing is appropriate and build in differentiation.

Simple substitution ⟶ **Significant rewrite**
(hug closely) (be adventurous)

With young children change class map then draw and retell before shared writing.

Create the right learning atmosphere – encourage creativity – "All ideas are accepted."
Create a learning routine:

- Innovation is underpinned by daily word and sentence games
- And daily shared and guided writing (the children should do some reading and writing every day)
- Include daily on-screen feedback to model how to reflect on what works
- Encourage children to reflect on their learning

Key teaching point for shared writing

Prepare thoroughly for shared writing

- write a version out first including your key learning points
- list your key learning points (based on cold task) so you remember to focus on them
- make the learning crystal clear – eg highlight features
- integrate grammar teaching into the process
- end session with children explaining what they have learnt

Make the learning visible

Use a washing line to display:

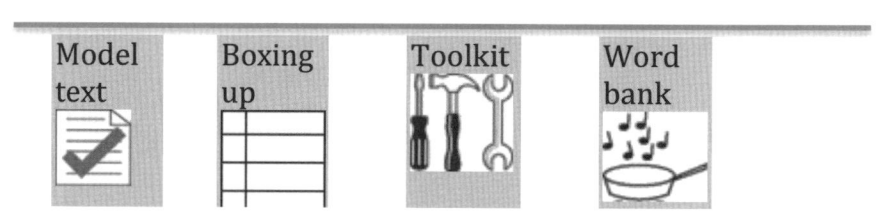

Model text	Boxing up	Toolkit	Word bank

Marking and feedback

Create an 'everyone will succeed' atmosphere – fear is the enemy of creativity. No one likes being judged
Use response partner approach and train the children to be constructive – to be true critical friends

Focus on the effect not the level or disembodied skills
Remember that the teachers have to know what good writing looks like
Always get the children to read their writing aloud so they hear it

What is helpful:

- Be positive – initially focus on what worked well
- Respond sensitively and personally as a reader and then as a writer and comment on how effects have been achieved
- Then focus on what needs improving
- Encourage children to jot down learning points
- Teach by illustration SHOW how to improve
- Be fussy – insist on what you have taught

"Think like a writer not a summative leveler."

"You can't 'upskill' a sentence – a sentence's quality depends on its context."

Analyse teacher comment in your school and who is doing all the work:

Where is the marking on this continuum?
Secretarial ⟶ composition & effect
Shift the focus from *secretarial* to *quality of composition* but don't forget the secretarial – sort secretarial features early on so increasingly the focus is on composition.
Over time the teacher should do less and the children more.
TEACHER ⟶ CHILDREN
DEPENDENCE ⟶ INDEPENDENCE

"Marking is your punishment for not involving the children in the process."

Involve the children in the process

- Remember what it feels like to have your work commented on
- Model for children (using real text on screen) how to reflect on their work
    - Read text aloud and hear the impact
    - what is effective and why?
    - what needs improving and how?
    - involve the children – put them in teacher role
- Ask the learner what approaches help them.
- Create a dialogue about how the child can progress so that, over time, each child can begin to independently assess how to progress
- Marking enables teacher to reflect on how effective their teaching has been as well as to focus on what needs to be taught to achieve progress.
- Marking should lead to immediate improvement

MARKING ⟶ FEEDBACK ⟶ IMPROVEMENT

"Feedback should be threaded through the whole unit."

Independent application

Before taking the scaffolding away altogether, use formative assessment to decide which aspects need revisiting and provide support – possibly mini lessons so that children are involved in selecting which aspects they need most.

Then set the **HOT TASK** – opportunity for children to show what they have learnt.

Then compare the COLD TASK with the HOT TASK: this enables:

- The teacher to
    - evaluate the effectiveness of their teaching
    - assess each child's progress
    - what needs focusing on in future units – use assessment to feed forward
- The child to see what progress they have made and what areas may need to be focused on next
- Parents to see the progress their child is making
- Senior management to monitor progress and have progress to show Ofsted

Use publishing as the [carrot] to motivate children to progress.

© Pie Corbett & Julia Strong www.talkforwriting.com
This resource may be reprinted to support in-school training but should not be used for commercial gain.

Handout 5a

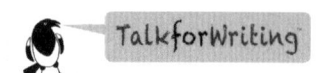

Boxing up the structure of the key story types (KS1)

There are only a few underpinning story types – some would argue there are as few as 6. This resource illustrates the pattern of the 8 key story types listed below.

1. Wishing stories
2. Warning stories
3. Beating-the-monster stories
4. Journey stories – quests, adventures
5. Losing stories
6. Suspense stories
7. Fantasy stories
8. Cinderella or change stories

Once children understand the underpinning structure of how stories work, they can create their own stories much more easily.

With younger children in Reception and Year 1 it is best to keep things simple and help them understand that every story has a beginning, a middle and end. Using story maps and story mountains to illustrate the structure with young children, helps them see the shape of the story.

By Year 2, children should be ready to see that stories typically have five parts:

- **Opening**
- **Build up**
- **Problem**
- **Resolution**
- **Ending**

This resource shows how the structure of these 8 types of stories can be boxed up into a simple grid to show the underpinning structure of the story.

1. Boxed-up structure for *Wishing tales* (KS1)

Sections/paragraphs		Key generic points	Innovation Key points
Beginning	**Opening**	• Main character out and about playing	
	Build-up	• Main character helps someone in trouble	
Middle	**Problem**	• Main character granted wish as reward • Main character makes wish • Wish turns out to be bad idea	
Ending	**Resolution**	• Main character overcomes the difficulty	
	Ending	• Main character reflects on his/her actions and learns a lesson	

2. Boxed-up structure for *Warning tales* (KS1)

Sections/paragraphs		Key generic points	Innovation Key points:
Beginning	**Opening**	• Two main characters told not to do something (go to a certain place)	
	Build-up	• They go out to play but decide to go to forbidden place	
Middle	**Problem**	• Something goes wrong	
Ending	**Resolution**	• Rescue!	
	Ending	• They get told off!	

3. Boxed-up structure for *Beating the monster* stories (KS1)

Sections/paragraphs		Key generic points	Innovation Key points:
Beginning	**Opening**	• Two characters happily playing outside	
	Build-up	• Something horrible comes along, e.g. bully, savage dog, dragon, goblin	
Middle	**Problem**	• Both characters run/hide	
Ending	**Resolution**	• They trick monster/manage to defeat monster	
	Ending	• All is well again • Main characters are proud of their deeds • They reflect on their bravery	

4. Boxed-up structure for Journey stories (KS1)

Sections/paragraphs		Key generic points	Innovation Key points
Beginning	**Opening**	• Main character given task	
	Build-up	• Main character begins journey with friend	
Middle	**Problem**	• Different events happen on way (3 events getting worse each time)	
Ending	**Resolution**	• Obstacles overcome with help of friend	
	Ending	• Main character and friend arrive and complete task • Main character thinks about what has happened. • Main character grateful for friend's help	

5. Boxed-up structure for *Losing tales* (KS1)

Sections/paragraphs		Key generic points	Innovation Key points
Beginning	**Opening**	• Main character has something precious	
	Build-up	• Main character sets off with precious item	
Middle	**Problem**	• Main character loses precious item • Main character searches everywhere	
Ending	**Resolution**	• Main character meets some friends who help him/her find precious item	
	Ending	• Main character finds safe place to keep item and vows to be more careful in future	

6. Boxed-up structure for Suspense/scary tales (KS1)

Sections/paragraphs		Key generic points	Innovation Key points
Beginning	**Opening**	• Main character playing	
	Build-up	• Main character hears/sees something out of place	
Middle	**Problem**	• Main character hides/runs but whatever it is, gets closer …	
Ending	**Resolution**	• Turns out to be something quite ordinary	
	Ending	• Main character relieved	

7. Boxed-up structure for *Fantasy tales* (KS1)

Sections/paragraphs		Key generic points	Innovation Key points
Beginning	**Opening**	• Main character goes to end of rainbow	
Middle	**Build-up**	• Main character finds something magical, e.g. a unicorn	
	Problem	• Something goes wrong	
Ending	**Resolution**	• Magic helps them	
	Ending	• Main character returns home	

8. Boxed-up structure for *Cindarella/change* stories (KS1)

Sections/paragraphs		Key generic points	Innovation Key points
Beginning	**Opening**	• Main character (creature) has a problem eg being sad, lonely, poor	
	Build-up	• Main character meets someone who needs help.	
Middle	**Problem**	• Main character helps.	
Ending	**Resolution**	• The main character is given a reward.	
	Ending	• Main character changed as result – no longer sad/lonely/poor etc.	

© Pie Corbett & Julia Strong www.talk4writing.com
This resource may be reprinted to support in-school training but should not be used for commercial gain.

Handout 5b

Boxing up the structure of the key story types (KS2)

There are only a few underpinning story types – some would argue there are as few as 6. This resource illustrates the pattern of the 8 key story types listed below.

1. Wishing stories
2. Warning stories
3. Beating-the-monster stories
4. Journey stories – quests, adventures
5. Losing stories
6. Suspense stories
7. Fantasy stories
8. Cinderella or change stories

By KS2, children should be very familiar with the underpinning structure of these 8 key story types and be ready to understand how the five-part opening, build up, dilemma, resolution ending structure can be varied. They will increasingly be shown how these patterns can be altered so that some stories combine element of different story types.

This resource illustrates how the boxed-up structure can be embellished to show the key elements of the five stages.

1. Boxed-up structure for *Wishing tales* (KS2)

Sections / paragraphs	Key generic points	Innovation Key points
Opening	• Main character (MC) wants something badly	
Build-up	• MC decides to try to get it • MC works out plan of action	
Dilemma/ problem	• MC prevented by some sort of difficulty • MC has to overcome this difficulty	
Resolution	• MC eventually gets what he /she wanted	
Ending	• Review of whether it was all worth it • Has MC been taught a lesson? • Will things be different now?	

2. Boxed-up structure for *Warning tales* (KS2)

Sections / paragraphs	Key generic points	Innovation Key points
Opening	• Two main characters warned not to do something	
Build – up	• They set off in spite of warning • They are tempted (one may be reluctant but gets dragged along) • They do what they have been warned against	
Dilemma/ problem	• Something goes wrong and they are in deep trouble • One gets free and goes for help • The other waits, desperately	
Resolution	• They are rescued and told off for breaking warning	
Ending	• Characters consider the consequences of their actions • Have they been taught a lesson? • Have their characters changed?	

3. Boxed-up structure for *Losing tales* (KS2)

Sections / paragraphs	Key generic points	Innovation Key points
Opening	• Main character (MC) given something	
Build-up	• MC uses/goes off with gift	
Dilemma / problem	• MC realises gift lost • MC searches in vain for lost item • MC returns home to face consequences	
Resolution	• Later, MC finds gift in unexpected place	
Ending	• MC shows his/her feelings • MC reflects on events and provides moral	

4. Boxed-up structure for *Suspense tales* (KS2)

Sections / paragraphs	Key generic points	Innovation Key points
Opening	• Main character (MC) is happily doing something	
Build - up	• MC hears, sees or senses something or someone ominous/scary	
Dilemma/ problem	• More scary things happen or are seen, MC reacts – runs/hides	
Resolution	• MC discovers what happening	
Ending	• MC shows his/her feelings • MC reflects	

5. Boxed-up structure for *Beating-the-monster tales* KS2)

Sections / paragraphs	Key generic points (Could be a dragon, ogre, savage dog, bully, storm, disease etc)	Innovation Key points:
Opening	• Setting created • All is well and happy with main characters (MCs)	
Build –up	• Image of MCs having good time in chosen place created	
Dilemma/ problem	• Monster introduced • MCs faced with monster • MC's lives change for worse	
Resolution	• MCs make plan to defeat monster • MCs manage to overcome monster	
Ending	• All well again after the defeat of monster • MCs show their feelings and reflect on events • MCs look to future	

6. Boxed-up structure for *Quest stories* (KS2)

Sections / paragraphs	Key generic points	Innovation Key points
Opening	• Main character (MC) & friend given task • MC prepares for journey	
Build-up	• MC sets off on journey	
Dilemma /problem	• On the way, something small goes wrong • This is overcome • Something worse happens in another place, but is overcome • Something even worse happens further on, but is overcome	
Resolution	• MC gets there in end • Main goal achieved	
Ending	• MC shows his/her feelings • This indicates how his/her character has changed • MC reflects on events and shows what has learned	

7. Boxed-up structure for *Change stories* (KS2)

Sections / paragraphs	Key generic points	Innovation Key points
Opening	• Main character (MC) is in a poor situation, e.g. lonely, sad, penniless, hungry, etc	
Build-up	• MC sets off to do something or go somewhere, seeking help	
Dilemma / problem	• MC comes across someone else who needs help	
Resolution	• Despite the disadvantage, MC helps	
Ending	• MC usually rewarded – the original problem is solved, e.g. they find a friend	

8. Boxed-up structure for *Fear stories* (KS2)

Sections / paragraphs	Key generic points	Innovation Key points
Opening	• Main character (MC) is afraid of something • MC gets teased about this	
Build - up	• MC starts to do something	
Dilemma / problem	• What the MC fears actually happens	
Resolution	• MC overcomes the fear	
Ending	• MC reflects on the events • MC pleased to have overcome the fear • MClooks to the future	

© Pie Corbett & Julia Strong www.talk4writing.com
This resource may be reprinted to support in-school training but should not be used for commercial gain.

| Handout 6 |

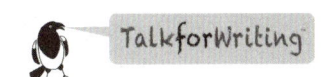

Model text

Little Red Riding Hood

Once upon a time, there was a girl called Little Red Riding Hood because she always wore a red coat with a bright red cap.

Early one morning, her mother said, "Take this basket of food to your grandmother but, whatever you do, don't dilly dally on the way." Into the basket, she put a slice of sweet fruitcake, a juicy apple and a large cheese.

So, Little Red Riding Hood walked and she walked and she walked until she came to the middle of the forest. The forest was dark and she could hardly see where she was going. Feeling tired, Little Red Riding Hood decided to rest under a huge tree. Suddenly, along came a woodcutter.

"Where are you going?" asked the woodcutter and Little Red Riding Hood told him.

Unfortunately, a grey wolf was hiding behind a tree, listening to everything they were saying. Greedily, it licked its lips, pawed the ground and ran off the find Grandma's cottage.

When Little Red Riding Hood reached Grandma's cottage, she let herself in. Grandma was lying in the bed but she looked very strange.

"What big ears you've got!" said Little Red Riding Hood.

"All the better for hearing you with," replied Grandma, sitting up.

"And what big eyes you've got!"

"All the better for seeing you with," replied Grandma, leaning forwards.

"And what big hands you've got!"

"All the better for hugging you with," replied Grandma, smacking her lips.

"And what big teeth you've got!"

"All the better for... eating you with!" shrieked the wolf, leaping from the bed.

Little Red Riding Hood screamed as the wolf opened its huge jaws.

Luckily, at that moment, the woodcutter dashed into the cottage and killed the wolf with not one, not two, but three, mighty blows from his axe! For, he had followed the wolf through the forest, tracked him to Grandma's cottage and arrived just in time.

Four leaf clover – our story is over.

© Pie Corbett: www.talk4writing.com
This resource may be reprinted to support in-school training but should not be used for commercial gain.

The Papaya that spoke

Once upon a time there was farmer who lived in a village. One day he felt hungry so he went out to pick a papaya. To his amazement, the papaya spoke, "Hands off!"

The farmer looked at his dog. "Did you say that?" said the farmer.
"No," said the dog, "it was the papaya!"
"Aaaaargh!" screamed the farmer. As fast as his legs could carry him, he ran and he ran and he ran till he came to a market where he met a fisherman selling fish.
"Why are you running so fast when the sun is shining so bright?" asked the fisherman.
"First a papaya spoke to me and next my dog!" replied the farmer.
"That's impossible," said the fisherman.
"Oh no it isn't," said one of the fish.

"Aaaaargh!" screamed the farmer. As fast as his legs could carry him, he ran and he ran and he ran till he came to a field where he met a shepherd with his goats.
"Why are you running so fast when the sun is shining so bright?" asked the shepherd.
"First a papaya spoke to me, next my dog and after that a fish!" replied the farmer.
"That's impossible," said the fisherman.
"Oh no it isn't," bleated one of the goats.

"Aaaaargh!" screamed the farmer. As fast as his legs could carry him, he ran and he ran and he ran till he came to the village where he met the King sitting on his old wooden rocking chair.
"Why are you running so fast when the sun is shining so bright?" asked the King.
"First a papaya spoke to me, next my dog, after that a fish and finally a goat!"
"That's impossible," said the King. "Get out of here you foolish man." So the poor farmer walked home with his head hung down. The King rocked back and forth, back and forth, back and forth. "How silly of him to imagine that things could talk." There was a long silence – and then suddenly – the chair spoke! "Quite so – whoever heard of a talking papaya?"

Retelling © Pie Corbett

The Red Eye

Outside, the wind howled across fens. Inside, the school was dark. Sally tiptoed down the corridor, slipped into the classroom and began to search for the map.

At that moment, the wind fell silent. Sally heard the door creak open. She ducked down behind the table, her heart thudding and her mind ablaze with questions. Silently, somebody came into the classroom. A red eye flickered. Who was it?

Pausing in the darkness, she began to think back to how she had ended up in such a mess. It had only been a few hours before when they had tidied up at the end of the school day. She had taken her father's antique map and, without thinking, put it onto Miss Simpson's desk for safekeeping.

Of course, she had forgotten to take the precious map home. Her Dad needed it for the next day and she knew that would mean a midnight escapade. So here she was, crouching in the darkness, her heart nagging with fear.

Without warning, the lights flicked on and she peered over the table, blinking like an owl. It was her brother Kevin and he had the map in his hand. "Come on," he hissed.

Ten minutes later, they were home. Dad had his precious map and was none the wiser, Kevin gloated and Sally lay tucked up in bed. Beyond the window, the darkness gathered, the storm died to a whisper and the empty street fell silent. Nothing moved in the darkness. Nothing stirred, except for a cold, red eye.

© Pie Corbett: www.talk4writing.com
This resource may be reprinted to support in-school training but should not be used for commercial gain.

Zelda Claw and the Rain Cat (longer version)
– short story to accompany the novel 'Varjak Paw' by SF Said

Thunder growled overhead. Zelda crouched in the darkness, staring. Wind lashed the glistening tarmac and the street lights flickered, casting shadows across the darkened road. Rusted dustbins rattled in the wind, fences creaked and the rain drummed on car roofs. Zelda shivered. Where could she escape from the downpour?

At that moment, Zelda sensed something crawling, something creeping along the pavement, hugging close to the shadows. Silently, a vague shape slipped into a doorway and Zelda was sure that she had glimpsed the flicker of a green eye. She could just hear a low growl even though the rain danced a thousand deaths on the pavement. Her fur prickled as she tensed herself. What was it?

Without thinking, Zelda ducked under a lorry and tucked herself into a space near the engine. It was still warm. She could just make out what looked like an enormous cat pacing through the rain, like a shadow moving silently along the rain washed pavements. Its white, needle-teeth jutted out of a scarlet mouth. Power surged through every step. Zelda flinched, crouching stiller than stone.

Beneath the lorry, Zelda waited but the great rain-cat drew closer and closer. Emerald eyes glittered crazily and Zelda could hear its claws scratching on the tarmac. Nearer it came until the great cat paused by the lorry's engine and sniffed. Could it smell Zelda's fear?

She could bear it no longer. Leaping out from under the lorry, Zelda shot back across the rain-swept road and leapt onto and over the wall. Landing the other side, she paused. Alone! The rain cat had not followed but Zelda could hear it screeching. And it was a sound that seemed to tear the night in half. Zelda shuddered with relief. She was safe – for now.

© Pie Corbett: www.talk4writing.com
This resource may be reprinted to support in-school training but should not be used for commercial gain.

Zelda Claw and the Rain Cat (shorter version)
– *short story to accompany the novel 'Varjak Paw' by SF Said*

All night, thunder growled overhead. Zelda crouched in the darkness, staring. Wind lashed the glistening tarmac and the street lights flickered, Zelda shivered. Where could she escape from the rain?

At that moment, Zelda heard something crawling along the pavement in the shadows. Silently, a vague shape slipped into a doorway. A green eye flickered. Zelda's fur prickled as she watched. What was it?

As a car purred by, the shadow of an enormous cat paced through the rain, moving silently along the rain washed pavements. Zelda crouched as still as stone.

Slowly, the great rain-cat drew closer and closer. Zelda could hear its claws scratching on the tarmac and see its green eyes glittering.

At that moment, Zelda could bear it no longer. Leaping out from under the lorry, she shot back across the rain-swept road and leapt over the wall. Now she was alone. The rain cat had not followed. Zelda was safe – for now.

© Pie Corbett: www.talk4writing.com
This resource may be reprinted to support in-school training but should not be used for commercial gain.

The Canal

"Now, I do not want you two playing down by the old canal. You know it's playing with fire," said Mrs Mac, digging her hands deep into the washing up bowl. Tom and Tiree nodded as if they understood.

Ten minutes later, they reached the old canal. Cautiously, they peered in. The water was still, black and deep. By the bank, they could see a rusted shopping trolley, old crisp packets and soggy newspapers. In the reeds, something rustled.

Although it looked dangerous, Tom grinned at his brother. He took the rope swing that dangled from an overhanging branch and leaped out over the canal. Swinging backwards and forwards, he whooped like a siren. Although Tiree was laughing, inside his heart was thudding. It was his turn next.

"You scared?" asked Tom, staring at him. Tiree did not want his brother to think that he was a coward so he ran back, leapt out and sailed across the canal. But half way over, the rope snapped. Tiree crashed down into the water. Tom gasped. Tiree was no swimmer!

Desperate, Tom leapt in. At first, he could see nothing – just darkness and weed tangling his feet. Then he saw red! It was Tiree's hoodie. Frantically, Tom grabbed it and tugged Tiree to the side. Tiree lay on the bank, gasping and wheezing like an old man.

Twenty minutes later, they were standing in Mrs Mac's kitchen. They had to explain what had happened and Mrs Mac grounded them for a week! After all, she had warned them often enough. The canal was dangerous. They had been lucky. This time.

© Pie Corbett: www.talk4writing.com
This resource may be reprinted to support in-school training but should not be used for commercial gain.

Ice Forest – *short story to accompany the novel 'Wolf Brother' by Michelle Paver*

It was late when Torak came to the ice forest. Tall trees towered over him, jagged with icicles that hung down like strange, sharp teeth. The last thin rays of winter sunlight slipped through the bare branches, casting a maze of ebony shadows on the forest pathway.

Torak sat down under a tree and waited. A bitter wind shivered through the forest, gripping his body in an icy fist. Torak sensed something moving in the dark; something watching him. He gripped a thin flake of flint and waited. A squirrel ran down a tree trunk, its beady eyes picking him out. Then it scurried back up and was lost into the treetops.

Far away, Wolf ran between the trees following the scent of Tall Tailless. In the distance, he could hear his brother's lonely call. A sharp, distant cry that drew him closer. Darkness settled onto the forest but Wolf loved the dark. Everything stilled and the scent track seemed cleaner and easier to follow. Stars glittered above and the moon hung like a bear's claw. He ran on.

Torak stared into the night so hard that his eyes ached. Something moved between the trees, pacing in his direction. Shivering, he tried to keep as still as rock, to become one with the tree. To be tree. A scuffle of leaves. The flicker of a branch. Torak longed for wolf whose night sight would soon seek out whatever was stalking him. The red eye had long gone. Now it was a world of shadows and shapes.

A snow-covered boulder seemed to rise out of the darkness. The ice bear stood on its hind legs. Its great face turned slowly, sensing the bitter stillness. Torak flicked the flint to one side and, as the bear moved towards the sound, he ran in the opposite direction.

Images whirled in Torak's mind. The ice bear's swollen eyes. The ice storm. Then he paused: silence; nothing. It were as if the forest had swallowed the bear. Something warm brushed by his leg. Wolf licked his hand – waiting to see what Torak would do next.

© Pie Corbett: www.talk4writing.com
This resource may be reprinted to support in-school training but should not be used for commercial gain.

116

Actions for 14 key linking words

Handout 7

First, ...	Next, ...	After that, ...	Later on, ...
Finally, ... Fortunately, ...	because ...	So... / so that...	Therefore, ... Unfortunately, ...
	Additionally, ...	For instance/example	
		but	also

© **Pie Corbett & Julia Strong** This resource may be reprinted to support in-school training but should not be forwarded to others or used for commercial gain.

Handout 8

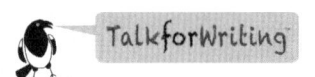

The art of linking text

Understanding the power of sentence signposts to link paragraphs, sentences, and information within sentences is key to achieving cohesive text that flows logically. They take the reader by the hand and guide them through the text somewhat like a sat nav guides a driver.

The term sentence signpost is a non-grammatical umbrella term to cover all the different structures used to guide a reader through a text. It includes the following grammatical structures:

1. **Co-ordinating conjunctions** (e.g. *and, but, or*). These are used to link the parts of sentences together, as in the following three-clause compound sentence: *The Dalek stared at the man **and** threatened to exterminate him **but** the man did not believe it.* Each clause is equally important.
2. **Subordinating conjunctions** (e.g. *because, if, since, although*). These are used to link two or more clauses within a sentence together, creating a main clause and one (or more) subordinate clauses, as in the following complex two-clause sentence: ***Although** the Dalek threatened to exterminate him, the man did not believe it.*
3. **Adverbials** – often at the front of sentences, hence the strange technical name 'fronted adverbial' (e.g. *However, Later that day, In addition*). These can be used to introduce a new paragraph or to link the sense of two separate sentences as in these examples:
    a) *The Dalek threatened to exterminate the man. **However**, the man did not believe it.*
    b) *The Dalek stared at the man and threatened to exterminate him. **Unfortunately**, the man did not believe it.*
   As with all adverbials, they don't have to stay at the front of the sentence but can move around within it but then, of course, they become just adverbials! They are, normally, marked off by commas:
    c) *The Dalek threatened to exterminate the man. The man, **however**, did not believe it.*
    d) *The Dalek stared at the man and threatened to exterminate him. The man did not, **unfortunately**, believe him.*
   A writer who wants to use them to guide the reader, usually puts them at the front of a sentence. If you throw them into the body of the sentence, they have more of an extra information role.
4. **Standard sentence structure beginning with a pronoun that refers back to whatever is being talked about to help the reader/listener follow the link succinctly.** E.g. *This led to …; It resulted in …,* as in the following simple sentence: ***This causes** the water to boil.*

Conjunctions (of the co-ordinating and subordinating variety) and fronted adverbials were covered by the umbrella-term *connective* in the National Strategy but the term connective is not mentioned in the New Curriculum because of the emphasis on using grammatical terminology. We use the term sentence signpost for any words and phrases that link text because it is useful for children to recognise the importance of using phrases that guide the reader or listener. As stated above, it is an umbrella term covering all the grammatical ways of linking text which are further illustrated below:

- **Co-ordinating conjunctions**: (e.g. *and, but, or*)
  *I like tea **and** chocolate **but** I don't like coffee.*
- **Subordinating conjunctions**: (e.g. *because, if, since*)
  *He felt nervous **because** an inspector had entered the room.*
- **Some fronted adverbials**: (e.g. *However, ... Unfortunately, ... The following day*)
  *The children cheered. **However**, one child felt very sad.*
- **Pronouns at the start of a sentence** referring back to earlier information: e.g.
  *The children cheered. **This** made one child feel very sad.*
- **Relative pronouns** (*e.g. who, that*) *Once, there was a boy called Charlie **who** lived in a big city.*

To write effectively, children need to know the difference between simple sentences (only one clause), compound sentences (more than one clause linked by co-ordinating conjunctions giving the clauses equal weight) and complex sentences (at least two clauses often linked by a subordinating conjunction, and always having a main clause and at least one subordinate clause). Children, therefore, need to understand the difference between the role of co-ordinating conjunctions and subordinating ones. When initially teaching co-ordinating conjunctions, it's best to focus on *and, but* & *or* as these are the ones that can only function as conjunctions.

It is worth pointing out that you can't really explain anything **without** using subordinating conjunctions **because** they show how one thing leads to another**, as** illustrated by the highlighted words in this sentence and its many clauses!

This is an important area and one in which understanding the grammar really makes a big difference. It is an area that often features on wall displays so it's important to get it right; otherwise greater confusion will ensue on all sides. We all need help with grammar; it is a tricky thing because context can change the function of words. It's worth having a grammar support group and helping each other teach grammar engagingly and accurately, supported by effective accurate grammar posters.

For a wide range of ideas on how to develop linking skills, see *Jumpstart! Grammar* – they hold the key to cohesive writing.

© Julia Strong: www.talk4writing.com
This resource may be reprinted to support in-school training but should not be used for commercial gain.

Handout 9

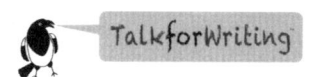

Shared writing talking frames – Pie's handy phrases

Phrases to encourage the children to strive to find the right word or phrase
(training the brain to generate alternatives and select the most appropriate) while not demotivating children by rejecting their ideas (fear is the enemy of creativity)

- We'll come back to that idea later
- That's not a bad idea
- Ooh, that would be a good word
- That's a lovely idea
- Lots of good ideas/ Lots of other good words
- I hope you use that
- Which do you think would work?
- We don't want…
- Our job as writers is to think of something new, something fresh that will startle the reader
- Think again
- That's a great idea
- Any others?
- See if you can get a list going
- Why do you think I chose that one?
- Let's go for…
- That's more dramatic

Phrases to encourage "magpie-ing" good words and phrases

- I hope you use that in your writing
- Let's bank that one
- I'm saving that one
- You can magpie from the model
- Jot some of the words down as we go along
- Ooh, save that good word
- Put that in the Save It bank
- Make certain you jot that down

Phrases to encourage looking more closely/ thinking/speaking further

- What else does it look like?
- Somebody give me something you can see/ hear
- What might you see?/hear?/feel?/think?
- Keep going
- What else could we have?
- Just think about that for a moment
- First thought not always the best thought
- Push, push, push. Are you pleased with…
- It's going to be much more powerful if
- Now let's think about this
- We don't want something so obvious

- We could say …… but I think we could do better than that
- Do you think we should say ….. or …..
- Can you say a little more about that

Phrases to encourage children to read sentences aloud to see if they work
- So just listen to this
- Reread it carefully
- Let's just read that and see how it sounds
- Let's reread it and that may help use do the next part

Phrases to help them use powerful nouns (name it)

- Do you know the name of a …

Phrases to add in extra challenges

- I'm going to do a simile now… As ------ as?
- Try some alliteration
- Now let's think about
- What word could we use to describe…

Getting everyone involved through talk partners

- Turn to your partner and… /finish that sentence off
- In fifteen seconds…
- On your whiteboards…
- In your pairs, quick…/ add a little more information

Keeping it pacy

I need the next sentence
Quick!" I need the next word

Understanding non-fiction texts

- What's this paragraph all about?
- Can you spot the topic sentence?
- How do you know this is the first/next/last paragraph?
- We need something else now
- We've got ---------- what else do we need? What could follow? You tell me.
- What facts would really interest the reader here?
- Now which bits of information are needed?
- Does it all fit together logically?
- Which bits don't seem to fit?
- What would make it flow better?
- How can we make the conclusion more interesting?

© Pie Corbett & Julia Strong   This resource may be reprinted for in-school training but should not be used for commercial gain.

The art of shared writing

Shared writing enables you to show the thought processes of a writer. Shared writing of spine poems is a great way in to help children refine the key writing techniques that will enable them to hook their reader and make their writing effective. Build on this in shared writing of all genre for fiction and non-fiction. Begin in reception and keep building so children automatically know how to use and adapt a wide range of techniques effectively.

Plan your shared writing
- Draft your shared writing so it clearly illustrates all the features you want the class to develop
- Integrate grammar meaningfully

Create the right ethos
- All ideas are accepted and valued – no wrong answers
- Encourage having a go
- Generate creative excitement and help them enjoy creative language
- Be enthusiastic: if you love it, they'll love it; if you're fussy, they're fussy

Make it interactive:
- Develop a range of techniques to involve the children:
    - *"In your pairs quickly …"*
    - *"On your mini white boards, …"*
    - Get everyone to join in
    - Give a range of choices for them to select from and make them explain their choices

Train children to generate ideas and vocabulary
- First thought not always the best – push, push, push for the most effective word or phrase.
- Don't write low level examples
- Experiment – try new combinations. If you've heard it before, it's a cliché
- Name it – add striking detail
- Never dodge a good word … use dotted line
- Discuss impact of choices – model thinking aloud as a writer
- Activate dormant language and introduce new words – act them out to demonstrate them
- Avoid empty terminology like "wow words"; name relevant grammar terms and integrate the grammar

Progressively model all the key writing techniques
- E.g. illustrate how to show not tell
- Spin sentences to show the possibilities: *the moon is like a claw – the moon is a claw – the clawed moon*
- Model the changes to see the process
- Use features (e.g. alliteration) to push for a new combination : *"Let's see if …"*
- *Give a weak example and then say it won't work well to promote better alternatives*

Train children to judge
- Model how a writer checks to see if their sentences work
- Keep re-reading to test if it works
- Oral rehearsal – say it aloud so can hear what works best
- Ask: *"Why does it work?"*
- Beware of 'overwriting' – reread for impact – demonstrate that less is often best
- Train them to magpie ideas from lessons and reading
- Jot down ideas – magpie from others

Make it visual
- Magpie ideas; bank ideas & learning points on washing line – use a save-it box/writers' notebooks

Keep it pacy
- But slow down for key moments - vary pace – pause for thought

Build confidence and enthusiasm
- Create the text together
- If you do shared writing well, the children will think they did it. It acts as a catalyst for their version.

Remember, the quality of the children's writing reflects the quality of your teaching
To improve your shared writing skills, get someone to film you; reflect on pace and process

© Pie Corbett & Julia Strong – TalkforWriting.com This resource may be reprinted for in-school training but should not be used for commercial gain.

Handout 11

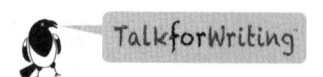

TalkforWriting

Teacher phrases supporting self assessment – helping the children to think and talk in a writerly way and use grammatical terms constructively

1. **Phrases to help students internalise the ingredients**

   - So what has made this bit so effective?
   - What could we call that?
   - How can we describe that?
   - Let's add that to our xxx toolkit.

2. **Phrases to help students talk about writing**

   - Jot down any phrase that you liked.
   - Tell me what helps makes this bit effective.
   - Look at the xxx toolkit. Can we see any examples here?
   - Keep going.
   - I love that idea.
   - Anything else?

3. **Feedback phrases to help children know what to do to improve**

   - First we want some good feedback.
   - What works?
   - What lines had a good effect on the reader?
   - Where's our best bit?
   - Where doesn't it sound right?
   - How can we improve it?
   - Are there any places where it jars?
   - What advice would you offer?
   - Anyone got any suggestions for how it might sound better?
   - What techniques were used that really worked?
   - How did it feel when you were reading my comments?
   - What would have helped you understand this better?
   - Who had a good response partner?
   - What made them good?

4. **Phrases to help children know how to improve their work**

   - In your pairs, which paragraph is better? What makes it better?
   - In your pairs, what advice would you give to this writer?
   - Are they equally good in different ways or is one better than the others?
   - Talk us through some of the sentences you've underlined and why you've focused on them?
   - What's the effect on the reader of that?
   - Let's hear somebody else's ideas.
   - What other things have we noticed?
   - Tell me more about why …

© Pie Corbett & Julia Strong: www.talk4writing.com
This resource may be reprinted to support in-school training but should not be used for commercial gain.

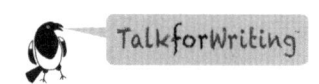

Different levels of innovation moving towards real independence

The original model text

"Now, I do not want you two fooling about down by the old canal. You know it's playing with fire," said Mrs Mac, digging her hands deep into the washing up bowl.
   Tom and Tiree nodded as if they understood.

Hugging closely

"Now, I do not want you two mucking about by the old warehouse. You know it's dangerous," said Mr Johnson, staring at the two girls.
   Gina and Geraldine smiled back as if they agreed.

Simple addition

"Now, I don't want you fooling around down by the old railway line. You know it's playing with dynamite," snapped Mr Jaggers, staring at the children.
   Tina and Tracey shuffled nervously as if they were already in trouble and promised that they would go straight home. Warily, Mr Jaggers watched as the two girls made their way across the playground. He sighed and, wearily, shook his head.

Sophisticated addition

Mr Jaggers peered over the rim of his spectacles at Tina and Tracey, as he put the note down. "Listen," he said kindly, "your Mum's worried that you'll not go straight home but I've told her that you'll be fine."
   The girls grinned, nodding their heads as if in agreement. Picking up their school bags, they left the classroom and set off for home. Blagger's Quarry was forbidden by their Mum but, today, she would be home late from work and it was their only opportunity …

Flashback start

It had only been a few hours beforehand when Mr Jaggers had warned them both not to go anywhere near Deathwatch Quayside. Again and again they had been told that it was dangerous. The wooden pier was unsteady. The water was deep. The currents were not to be trusted. They had been warned … but it had not been enough.

Sequel

You would have imagined that one warning was enough. But no – Tom had the devil in him. At least, that was what his Mother said. Tiree wanted nothing to do with this latest escapade. He'd been in enough trouble over the canal incident and did not want to be grounded yet again. But Tom was persuasive and, once again, Tiree found himself too far in to escape. Trouble seemed to be his second name.

© Pie Corbett: www.talk4writing.com
This resource may be reprinted to support in-school training but should not be used for commercial gain.